MW00981690

May these
encourage you in life's journey.

H.G.Wiebe   Proo. 3: 5-6

On the Sunny Side

Henry G. Wiebe

 FriesenPress

Suite 300 - 990 Fort St
Victoria, BC, V8V 3K2
Canada

www.friesenpress.com

Copyright © 2020 by Henry G. Wiebe
First Edition — 2020

Illustrations by Steven Roberts

All rights reserved.

No part of this publication may be reproduced in any form, or by any
means, electronic or mechanical, including photocopying, recording, or any
information browsing, storage, or retrieval system, without permission in
writing from FriesenPress.

ISBN
978-1-5255-7648-5 (Hardcover)
978-1-5255-7649-2 (Paperback)
978-1-5255-7650-8 (eBook)

1. RELIGION, CHRISTIAN LIFE, INSPIRATIONAL

Distributed to the trade by The Ingram Book Company

Table of Contents

Introductory Comments

For several years I submitted short, monthly articles to a local Okanagan newspaper. In 2015 the Oliver Daily News on-line newspaper requested a weekly uplifting and inspirational column from a Christian perspective. I named it *On the Sunny Side.* Admittedly, there are a few forays into the darker side.

Some people asked where the material for these Sunny Side articles came from. Do I sit down in front of a blank computer screen and wonder what would be a good choice for the next Sunny Side article? No, leaving that to deadline pressure is unwise. I need to have choices so that I am more likely to select the right article for that week. Here is the plan I use with reliance on the Lord for wisdom.

The Sunrise folder in my computer contains potential items in the idea or rough copy stage. These ideas come from experiences I encounter, things I notice while on walks, thoughts that I believe the Lord grants me, news items, magazine articles or clippings I have collected over many years plus ideas from books I read. Each one of the items in the Sunrise folder will need a fair bit of work to even be a possibility. Some are discarded in the process as being unsuitable. I have occasionally quoted from the source, or sources, and then given credit to the authors or publications. I extend my appreciation to them all, especially to the ones I contacted to obtain permission to use them as a source.

Once an article has been developed to the possibility stage it is moved into the Sunset folder. They all need a little more work to become suitable for publication, or at least somewhat suitable. The aim is to make them just right for the time of year and effective in the way they are written. I want them to be smart: Short, Meaningful. Appealing, Relevant and True. That is a tall order, seldom fully achieved. After submission the article joins the Sunny Side folder of currently more than 260 that have already been used. So that is the process and it is still going on.

For this I need help and wisdom. It's a good thing that James 1:5 promises: *"If any of you lacks wisdom, you should ask God, who gives generously to all without finding fault, and it will be given to you."*

Thank you, Lord!

Henry Wiebe

THEME 1

Attitudes

What should be my attitude towards the circumstances I am in?

"Rejoice always, pray continually, give thanks in all circumstances; for this is God's will for you in Christ Jesus." 1 Thessalonians 5:16-18

BLESSING

I am blessed because:

- I have more healthy days than sick ones,
- I am not living in a war zone,
- I am not facing starvation like many millions around the world do,
- I have enough money coming in regularly to get by, and
- I can read what follows unlike the hundreds of millions who can't read.

I have good reasons to maintain an attitude of gratitude.

BLIND LEADERS

An elderly lady was waiting to cross the street at the lighted intersection. Not being very steady on her feet, nor quick in her step, she double checked the traffic when the walk signal came on. By the time she began to step into the crosswalk the walk signal disappeared and she had to wait again. "I wish someone would help me get across the street," was her thinking. At that point a gentleman came along and asked, "May I take your arm as we cross the street?" She willingly agreed. Partway across the street the gentleman tripped and fell. "What happened?" asked the lady. "You'd almost think you were blind not to have seen that pothole." "I am almost blind," responded the man. "That's why I asked for your help. I'm trying to cope without my white cane."

Do we cry over a lost ability, laugh at the situation, get angry about an obstacle or just give in to using the cane? What is going to by my attitude about things that trouble me? Make the right choice. It's an imaginary story but real life for some.

Choose a helpful solution.

BUILDING OR WRECKING?

Most of us have watched a building being demolished. In a rather short period of time what may have taken months or years to build has been destroyed. Not only that, the skills that were needed to build it are much greater than the skills it takes to bring it down.

There's a lesson in that story. It is much easier to tear a person down than to build that person up. We are often so ready to criticize and complain rather than encourage and commend.

Have I walked life's road with sufficient care, measuring each deed with rule and square?

Or am I one who roams the town, content with the labor of tearing down?

COPING

In *Aug., 1997, I decided to prepare a series of sermons on how to cope when there seems to be no hope. It would be based on Peter's first epistle (in the New Testament). I sort of think that the Lord sat back and said, "Hmmm, so you want to talk to the people about coping, huh? What do you know about coping when there is no hope?"*

"Well, I..er..that is..well, my parents did not have much when I was growing up."

"Really? Did you ever not have enough to eat, or clothes to wear or a place to sleep?"

"No, we always had those. But after I got married we had 5 children, and I was a teacher and principal and then later a pastor. Doesn't that count?"

"Most of the time it was smooth sailing for you. You did not endure much persecution, tragedy, poverty, serious health problems, war or famine. When were you ever without hope?"

"Yes, I guess You are right."

"I think you need a little taste of what it means to cope before you try to tell your congregation anything."

Within a few days I was in an ambulance heading for the Intensive Care Unit in Penticton, BC. It was a small stroke (TIA). With encouragement and prayer support from many people I quickly recovered from a state of not being able to see straight, think straight, walk straight or talk straight. The balance and seeing took longer to come back but I only missed one Sunday away from the pulpit. Still seeing double, I told the congregation that the church had grown marvellously in my absence. With determined effort I regained balance and have been physically active since then.

Three weeks after the TIA we received a desperate phone call from our son, Steven, with the news that the doctors were expecting their premature, 2 day old son, Connor, to die that evening. The sight of him hooked up to multiple tubes and wires in an incubator hit grandma so hard she had to be helped out of the room.

However, Connor, who we thought would be physically and mentally handicapped if he survived, graduated from secondary school at or near the top of his class academically and has been very active in sports. He is also achieving high marks in electrical engineering at university. We have very much to be grateful for.

Thankful to be on the lighter side of coping challenges.

GRATITUDE

What would we think of a son or daughter who was provided with everything needed and then demanded more? How would we feel if that child used everything available for personal benefit and hardly ever did anything helpful in response nor ever expressed any appreciation? Would we put up with an attitude of entitlement when the child complained that he/she didn't get even more and better things?

Before we get very angry even thinking about such a scene, let us ask if we treat God that way. Every day I am at the receiving end of His goodness and grace. Do I take that for granted? Continually I am surrounded by opportunities galore, marvelous beauty and endless things to explore and discover yet do I complain if things don't go the way I want? Why would we think that there is no limit to what God will put up with? Thankfully He is a forgiving and compassionate God. What we need to do is show our appreciation by the way we treat our environment, other people and God Himself.

Walk on the sunny side.

GENUINE HUMILITY

The corporal of a small army squad was giving orders to his men to raise a timber to the top of a military building. The weight and size of the beam was making it hard for the men to lift it into place. Frequent commands to push, heave and try harder ensued. A passerby in civilian clothes asked the corporal why he didn't help them. With astonishment and a pompous attitude the man replied, "I am a corporal!"

"You are, are you?" responded the passerby, "I was not aware of that. I ask your pardon, Mr. Corporal." With that the stranger stepped up to the beam and helped the men lift it into place. As he was leaving the stranger said, "Mr. Corporal, when you have another such job and have not men enough, send for your **Commander-in-Chief,** and I will come to help you a second time." The passerby was General George Washington.

"...whoever wants to be great among you must be your servant..."
Matthew 20:26

Those who don't exalt themselves spend more time on the sunny side.

JUST IMAGINE

Martin was somewhat despondent about the lack of progress in his work. Restless and listless, nothing productive was coming together for him. To ease his frustration he went outside and just lay down on the grass, looking up at the sky. The fleecy clouds and blue sky had a calming effect. He began to be captivated by the movements and configurations of the patches of cloud. This one looked a bit like a lamb skipping across the sky. That one was an elephant, complete with a trunk. Over there a ship was ploughing through the ocean waves. One cloud covered the sun for a while, displaying a silver lining. Then what was that forming? Was it a face? It was as though Someone was telling him something. Don't give in to despair. Change your perspective. There are wonderful sights and great opportunities for enjoyment. Don't just fret over the evil and injustice in the world. Remember God's promise in John 10:10, *"I am come that they may have life, and have it to the full."* Martin went back to his work with a completely changed attitude.

It's brighter on the sunny side.

MUD OR STARS?

In his book, *Man of Character in a World of Compromise*, Richard Exley tells of a woman whose husband was posted to the army camp near the Mojave Desert, California. An excerpt from the story illustrates her attitude.

> *I loathed it. I had never before been so miserable. My husband was ordered out on maneuvers and I was left in a tiny shack alone. The heat was unbearable at 125 degrees. Not one person to talk to in English. The wind blew incessantly, and all the food I ate, and the very air I breathed, was filled with sand. I'd rather be in jail.*

She wrote her parents to say she was giving up and coming home. Her mother wrote back with only two lines.

Two men looked out from prison bars,
One saw the mud, the other saw the stars.

The young woman felt ashamed and made up her mind to look for the stars.

> *I made friends with the natives, showed interest in their weaving and pottery and they gave me presents of their favorite pieces. I learned about prairie dogs and desert sunsets. I was a changed person. The desert and my circumstances hadn't changed, but I had. I found the stars.*

Are we looking for the bright side?

ONE SELF-CENTERED LIFE

Imagine yourself as the sole owner of a huge manufacturing business. You were the only founder and builder of the company. Every employee was valued and placed according to ability where she/he

7

could have success. Each person was provided with the opportunity to establish a home and family where you provided the infrastructure, services and amenities to meet needs and to provide for enjoyment. The benefits they had were marvelous. You personally were committed to their well-being.

Imagine your reaction if I, as an employee, decided to ignore your instructions for the job and to build whatever I felt like doing. How would you feel if I used everything you had provided for my personal benefit and then complained if it wasn't the way I wanted it? What would your reaction be if I said that you had no right to criticize my actions because, after all, I was getting along with the rest of the employees? What would you say if I stated that you had no right to tell me what to do because I don't believe you made all this? It just came about by itself. You are pretending to be the owner.

If I was that employee you would be right to criticize me for being extremely self-centered. Might it be that in my pursuit of what's interesting for me I'll find 'me' not interesting, and worse, expendable? This is how many treat the Creator of our universe and yet He still says, "I love you." He really does care for you. John 10:10 *"I have come that you may have life and have it to the full."*

We can choose the sunny side.

PSALMS

For nearly a year I concentrated on a study of the psalms in my daily devotions. After completing that adventure I came to the following conclusions.

The psalms express both the heart-cry of mankind in his search for God and his heart-throb when he finds Him. They contain the full range of feelings as people express themselves to God and the full range of God's responses. Both of these span the spectrum of reactions from full-blown anger to overwhelming love. The psalms paint a picture of what a relationship with God can be like. Woven into the record is an acknowledgment of our humanness. All the emotional roller-coasters, the celebrations of praise, the mental anguish, the displays of power and the bouts of despair are reflected.

The psalms affirm the various ways in which people relate to God.

The **contemplative** person listens and loves to be alone with the Lord.

The **aesthetic** admires the beauty of His creation and perfection of His ways.

The **activist** is committed to doing things, to be working for the Lord.

Relational people express love to others and enjoy the Lord as a Friend.

Demonstrating joy, acting out emotions, and displaying our worship in physical actions is the exuberant arena of the **experiential** person.

Tucked away in a den somewhere is the **studious** believer, discovering jewels of truth in the mine of God's Word.

All of these are found in the psalms. No wonder they are the most read portion of the Bible no matter what your attitudinal perspective on life is.

ROCK HOUNDS

Rock hounds have been known to devote hours to collecting rocks they sense have qualities brighter than their drab outer appearance.

A story is told about a lone man in a mountain cabin who was using an unusual rock as a doorstop. He didn't recognize it as a large gold nugget. If it was a precious stone instead of gold, its value would become evident by cutting and polishing until that cut surface displayed a beauty in color and radiance that would transform its appearance.

In a somewhat similar way remarkable traits in people can surface during critical times. We are told in several places in Scripture that we need to endure the positive disciplinary processes that Lord sends our way because they are intended to be the means for bringing out the beauty of refined qualities. We may chafe under the cutting, grinding and polishing but the Lord patiently continues His work on us because He can already see the desired end product. The big difference between us and the rock is that we have a will, emotions and a mind of our own. The rock has no choices and no feelings. But if we rebel at what the Lord wants to teach us we will sorely regret that response because that comes with consequences. Our attitude will make the difference.

There is another way in which a rock can be precious. In Scripture Jesus is compared to a solid rock in several places. He provides a firm foundation for life. A shipwreck on the Atlantic seaboard left a young lad as the only survivor. Pounding waves dumped him onto a rock to which he clung all night. When rescued in the morning by the coast guard he was asked if he had been frightened. His answer was that he had trembled all night but the rock did not tremble.

Grateful for solid footing.

STARTLING CHANGE

Alexander Rostovtsev was a popular comedian and matinee idol in Russia years ago. He was enlisted to play the part of Jesus in a blasphemous comedy titled *Christ in a Fur*. The first act showed the inside of a church building where the altar was like a bar displaying various liquors. Attendees dressed as nuns or clergy were at gambling tables or even staggering around nearly drunk. Rostovtsev had a reputation for being a sneering enemy of Christ, a disciple of Marx and an avowed opponent of Christianity. His part was to begin with the reading of the first two verses of Matthew 5, then throw off his oriental robe and shout, "Give me instead my furs and top hat!"

He read the first verse. *"Blessed are the poor in spirit: for theirs is the kingdom of heaven."* Then he suddenly stopped as if paralyzed. The audience that had roared and cheered when he walked onto the stage were now gripped with an uneasy silence. The actor's body was shaking. He started reading again, and kept on reading out loud. Back stage the prompter tried to get his attention so they could urge him to follow the script, but to no avail. He read to the end of the chapter and then cried out, "Lord, remember me when thou comest into thy kingdom." Management lowered the curtain, cancelled the rest of the performance and announced that Rostovtsev had suddenly become very ill. It is more likely that he had suddenly found spiritual health. He was not heard from again.

Sources: Feb. 14, 1964 devotional article in Our Daily Bread; Richard Wurmbrand's book "Tortured for Christ"; and the internet.

YUSUF LOSUTO

When I am tempted to complain about the inconveniences and destructive consequences of the current health and economic crises,

I am wise to remember the following personal encounter during the year we were in Africa.

When my wife and I were in Kijabe, Kenya on a one-year short term mission, Yusuf was a student in one of my classes at Moffat Bible College. Some students would typically invite the teacher to come to their villages for a weekend. It would include visiting and preaching. I would gladly go every time I was asked, so when Yusuf invited me I agreed to go. I might have hesitated had I known the background to his story.

At age 12 his job was to be the goat herder for his father. The Pokot tribe Yusuf was born into was a nomadic tribe in a remote area of Kenya. Life was very difficult due to poverty, semi-desert conditions and tribal conflicts. Yusuf and 6 other goat herders his age were attacked by Turkana rustlers on horseback. The boys had spears, the Turkana had guns. Yusuf managed to hide under a bush. The other 6 were killed.

Understandably, Yusuf pleaded with his father to let him go to school instead of herding goats. His father refused because school wouldn't make him a better goat herder. Yusuf didn't want to herd goats – also understandable – so he ran away to a school run by missionaries. The father came to haul him back home but Yusuf fled again. This time the father threatened to kill him if he ran away again. "You won't have to," declared Yusuf. "I'll just commit suicide." The mother intervened and Yusuf got to go to school when a missionary agreed to pay for it. He started school at age 12 in a language (English) that he didn't know. He stuck it out, graduated, became a Christian and was now (1992) a student at Moffat with the goal of going back to his tribe as a pastor. By this time the father's attitude had mellowed.

Yusuf the Pokot, Biwot the Kalenjin, Dixon the Maasai and John the Kikuyu piled into my car. After the pavement and the gravel road petered out we drove through wilderness until the acacia thorn bushes prevented further progress. We passed a gravesite where Yusuf's grandfather was buried. He was a Pokot hero for killing 100 Maasai enemies. I have a picture of Yusuf and Dixon shaking hands over his grave. We walked until we spotted beehive-shaped huts that served as this clan's living quarters. I say 'clan' because the father had 4 wives and more than 16 children based on a group photo I have. Each wife had her own hut that she had constructed herself, a 2-day project each time they moved unless a previously built hut was still there. A tree branch cot with a goat skin was the bed, 3 stones served as the kitchen fireplace and a few 'tools' and a spear hung on the wall. Some metal cups and a plastic pail told me it was the 20th century, not the 15th. At the father's command the whole clan gathered to listen to this white man, a rare guest. Some were visibly reluctant.

The idea of a Creator is generally accepted in these tribes so I briefly traced the story from creation to the cross, with Yusuf as interpreter. The focus was on God's loving provision and forgiveness. There followed traditional expressions of thanks to the guest.

Then Yusuf and his brother brought a goat to me and asked if it was good enough. Puzzled, I said it certainly was but Yusuf decided to get a better one. There in front of me, while one person lifted the front legs, Yusuf plunged a spear into the goat's heart, caught the blood in a bowl, and brought the goat to the women for meal preparation.

The men and some of the boys went for a walk where I saw a pond available to cattle and wild animals. This was the better source of water. A green algae covered the brown water in a slough that was the other option. The meal was delicious except for the chai made of tea and either goat's milk or camel's milk. I had seen the water source but refusing hospitality was a great insult.

Within one hour after the 6 hour trip back to Kijabe I became really sick for three days. I believe it was the Lord who kept me healthy long enough to drive back. There was no other driver. Two weeks later I went on another ministry trip with a different student. I wanted to do what I could during the one year I was there.

THANKSGIVING AFTERTHOUGHTS

Many of us have had great Thanksgiving weekends. Time with family and a scrumptious turkey dinner are hard to beat. But I got to thinking about this.

We praise the cooks for their skill in producing a delicious meal, and so we should. But what about the One who created the vegetables, the turkey, the fruit and all the other ingredients? Did He get any thanks?

We use a computer and marvel at the genius of the people who worked for years to bring it to where it is now. That is a well-deserved honor. But who was it that put the potential for electronic data storage and transfer into the microchips used? Certainly not us. Does the Lord get any recognition?

All of us have enjoyed musical numbers that resonate with our preferred genre. The musicians and singers are skilled and deserve credit. But who created the very possibility for music and song to exist? Who gave wood and metal the potential for producing wonderful sounds? Do we give Him the faintest thought?

No wonder that these, and dozens of other examples, have caused the Scriptures to say, *"For although they knew God, they neither glorified him as God nor gave thanks to him…" Romans 1:21.*

Thanks be to God for graciously blessing us with a marvelous array of potential.

WELCOME HOME

President Theodore Roosevelt disembarked from his ship at a San Francisco dock. He was coming home from a hunting safari in Africa and crowds lined the route as he walked off the ship. There was cheering, ringing of bells, whistles and a red carpet on the pier. A huge amount of fanfare greeted the president.

Another gentleman disembarked from the ship, worn out, old and gray after spending most of his life serving as a missionary in Africa. His wife had died, his children had gone elsewhere and communication wasn't as easy or effective then as now. No one was there to greet him as he came home. Somewhat despondent he made his way to a small hotel where he could spend the night. In his heart he was thinking, "Lord, I gave my life for You in Africa but no one seems to care. Mr. Roosevelt goes there for a few weeks of holidays and people go wild with welcoming him home. I don't understand."

It seemed as though the Lord responded with, "Son, wait a bit longer. You're not home yet."

THEME 2

Christmas

What's so great about the good
news at Christmas?

*"I bring you good news that will cause great
joy for all the people." Luke 2:10*

A CHRISTMAS PRAYER

Lord Jesus, I want to rise above the hustle and bustle of the Christmas activities. I seek that quiet place where I can meditate on what it was like for You to leave heaven and come to planet earth as a baby.

May I be more like those who recognized that there was something very special happening in the manger. May I not be like those who walked past with no idea of what this was all about.

May I say with Mary, *"My soul glorifies the Lord."* Luke 1:46-47.

CHRISTMAS EVE MARVEL.

The year was 1862, during the Civil War. It was a bitter cold night, with bright moonlight that gave a clear view to everything below. A Confederate soldier was on picket duty when across the field a Union soldier, who was also on picket duty, came into full view. The Confederate soldier got his musket and took aim, completely hidden in the shadows. Just as he did, the Union soldier began to sing.

Saviour, like a shepherd lead us, much we need thy tender care.
In thy pleasant pastures feed us, for thy use our folds prepare.
Blessed Jesus, blessed Jesus, Thou hast bought us thine we are.
Blessed Jesus, blessed Jesus. Thou hast bought us, Thine we are.

This took the soldier with the musket by surprise. He thought to himself, "I'll let him finish his song, then I'll shoot him. I can't miss him and he won't be able to get away fast enough." At that moment, the singing soldier started verse two:

"We are Thine, do Thou befriend us, BE THE GUARDIAN OF OUR WAY".

The music touched his heart as he heard it and he took his finger off the trigger. It brought back childhood memories of when his mother would sing that song to him, teaching him of the Lord. He listened until the end of the song, then dropped his musket. Without the Union soldier ever knowing he had been there, he turned and slipped away into the darkness.

Fourteen years passed, and it was now 1876. The Union soldier had since become a very well-known hymn writer and song leader, traveling with Evangelist D.L. Moody. His name was Ira D. Sankey. He had written many hymns and also composed the music to many other famous hymns like *A Shelter in the Time of Storm*. He was on his way home, on a steamboat on the Delaware River on Christmas Eve. Many passengers on board recognized Sankey and decided they would ask him to sing a song for everyone. On the deck, Sankey agreed and leaned against one of the big funnels. He paused for a moment, before he started. He wanted to sing a Christmas song, but the Lord seemed to lead in another direction. The words to *Saviour, Like A Shepherd Lead Us* came to his mind and he felt impressed to sing this song. So, he did. Everyone on deck listened intently to the singer, and the words of the song. The Lord's power was on him and his song.

As he finished, a bearded man approached Sankey from the other side of the deck. He asked Sankey if he could speak with him for a moment. As the two men separated from the crowd, the bearded stranger asked Sankey if he had ever served in the Union Army. Sankey replied with the answer of yes. The stranger asked if he had picket duty, 14 years ago, on a clear cold night. Sankey said yes, and asked if the stranger had been there in service also. He told him yes, but had been a Confederate soldier. He went on to tell Sankey he had seen him in clear view, while hidden in the shadows across the enemy lines. He told him how he had raised his musket to fire, and at that same moment he had begun to sing. "It was the same song you sang tonight. When I heard your voice, I knew it was you."

He went on the tell Sankey how he planned on letting him finish his song, and then shoot him. "When you started to sing the part that said, "We are Thine, do thou befriend us, be the Guardian of our way...", it touched my heart. It made me think of my dear mother who had passed away, and how she loved the Lord, and would sing this same song to me as a child. I couldn't shoot you. My heart was smitten. I didn't know what to do, so I slipped off in the darkness. These fourteen years I have often thought of that night.

Tonight, I know that the Lord was able to save you from certain death, and was the Guardian of your way. He MUST SURELY be great and mighty. I have wandered these fourteen years since then, lost without that Shepherd. Will you please tell me how he can save me?"

And there, on board that steamboat, two soldiers, once enemies, now prayed together for that Great Shepherd to bring another lost sheep home.

(Check the internet to verify: Sankey Civil War)

WAS IT AN EMPTY CHRISTMAS?

Empty is not a word normally associated with Christmas. We don't want to even think of emptiness. We want piles of gifts under the tree, a house full of family and friends, full stockings and full stomachs. We want to be full of joy and good cheer. Tragically, some did have to cope with empty stomachs, empty places at the table, empty wallets and empty hearts. However, there are also some very significant, positive empty things connected with this season.

19

Christ emptied himself

The account in Philippians 2:7 tells us that when Jesus came to earth *"He made Himself nothing, taking the very nature of a servant"*. This is very difficult to understand. How could the God of the universe take the form of a man and do that? It is even more stupendous than having a king, president or prime minister take the place of a slave laborer voluntarily. We want to be a **somebody,** not a **nobody**. But He made Himself nothing for us.

The manger is empty

We love the picture of an innocent baby in the manger. It is an awesome scene but we can't keep Him there. Our natural inclination would be to have Him stay there. After all, it is much cuter and more comfortable to deal with baby Jesus than the thundering Prophet or the probing Teacher who pierces our thoughts, challenges our hypocrisy and cuts across the cords of our culture. But the manger is empty. God's visit to earth was not going to be just a cute social event in which we could "ooh" and "aah" over a baby and then go on our way undisturbed. He came to intervene and even interfere. He came to comfort and console but also to confront and convict. We are sorely mistaken if our only mental image of God is that of a doting grandfather or of the Son of God as a cute baby. The manger is empty now.

The cross is empty

The cross has a lot to do with Christmas. You see, He came to die not just to visit. They couldn't leave Him in the manger where He wouldn't challenge us, so they decided to nail Him to the cross where He couldn't interfere, they thought. But He rose again when all seemed to be black with hopeless defeat. He continues to reach out to mankind with even greater hope. He came to die so that we might have life. (John 10:10)

Many hearts are empty

Although the days were scheduled full, the dinner tables were full and the space under the tree loaded with gifts, many hearts were still very empty. Somehow the conviction pierces through the busyness, the festivity and the materialism with the thought that this really isn't fulfilling. There is something missing. There is a great emptiness in there somewhere. Jesus said, *"Come to Me, all you who are weary and burdened, and I will give you rest."* Matthew 11:28 May we each experience that a personal relationship of faith in the Lord Jesus Christ is the only thing that can fill that emptiness. Life is full on the sunny side.

GOD KEEPS PROMISES

Christmas is a time when hope runs high. Children expect gifts they asked for. Adults wish that peace and love would reign. Many promises and resolutions are made for the New Year. Each year many of those expectations turn into empty promises.

However we can count on God to keep His promises. The promised birth of Jesus, the Messiah, is the focal point of the season for Christians. Many do not realize how long ago God first promised that a Redeemer would come nor how many seemingly impossible hurdles stood in the way. It was a promise to Adam and Eve that this Messiah would be sent. (Gen. 3:15) When the first two sons were born Eve thought one of them would surely fill that role, but when Cain murdered Abel that hope was dashed.

Abraham was promised a son through whom this Promised Son would eventually arrive but he was already 99 and his wife 89 with no son in sight. But Isaac did come. Grandson Jacob had twelve sons and one of them would begin the lineage through which the Messiah would come. Their behavior hardly was the kind that would encourage us to believe that would happen because they sold brother Joseph into slavery. God had warned Abraham that his descendants would be slaves in a foreign country for 400 years (Gen. 15:13). Just when it was time for a deliverer to rescue the Israelites from slavery in Egypt, Pharaoh decided to have all baby boys killed to avert the danger of revolt. Most of us know about the rescue of baby Moses from the Nile by the daughter of Pharaoh. Ironically, while seeking to avert the rise of a leader to deliver the Israelites he was raising him in his own palace. God keeps promises in spite of impossible odds.

A similar situation developed when finally the Promised Messiah was to be born. Herod massacred the male babies in Bethlehem but Joseph and Mary escaped to Egypt with baby Jesus. God continues to keep promises.

Ultimately the Jewish religious leaders in collusion with the Romans thought they could rid themselves of Jesus by crucifying Him, but that very action was the means by which God offers salvation to us. Even when things look impossible, God keeps His promise. We can sing with confidence, "Go, tell it on the mountain...that Jesus Christ is born."

The sunny side is very promising.

DOES GOD CARE?

"Peace on earth, good will to men". **Does God really care what happens on planet earth?** There is so much crime, abuse and suffering. With the psalmist we might well ask, "*what is man that You are mindful of him, the son of man that you care for him?" Psalm 8:4* God does care, and it shows in at least 4 ways.

1. He made it a **priority** to visit our planet. Our position on a priority list determines how much we believe the other

person cares. Christmas is about God communicating with us in person.

2. The ones who care will be **honest** about our condition. When Jesus came He harbored no delusion about what He would find, nor did He hide the diagnosis. *"Christ Jesus came into the world to save sinners." 1 Timothy 1:15* Sin is real. It has to be dealt with.

3. The **price** we are willing to pay says how much we care. What price was God prepared to pay for a cure? That will tell us how much He cared. *"God so loved the world that He gave His one and only Son"* John3:16. *"Greater love has no man than this that a man lay down his life for his friend."* John 15:13 He was willing to pay the ultimate price. God cared a lot.

4. There is at least one more criteria for caring we must mention, **choice**. I can choose to accept or reject the treatment. The Bible clearly declares that whosoever will may come. God cares enough to give us the choice. After all He has provided He still allows us the opportunity to reject Him.

The promised Messiah of Christmas tells us that God cares a lot about each one of us. You matter to Him. We trust that you will **experience** the sunny side of God's loving care this Christmas season.

GOD'S GIFTS

At this season of the year we are urged to remember God's visit to earth in the person of Jesus. He was the epitome of God's statement to us according to Hebrews 1:1-3. If that was the ultimate communication, does He also speak to us in other ways?

1. Every day, everywhere to everyone He speaks through creation. As one example, when a microscopic sperm unites with a microscopic egg, a complete blueprint for an adult human being is put into place. After cell multiplication the stem cells diversify into many different muscle, nerve, skin, blood, flesh and brain cells. The different organs form. The complete blueprint, equivalent to a library of instructions, is contained in one microscopic cell. It's the DNA. We are indeed *"fearfully and wonderfully made" Psalm 139:14* The same kind of wonders exist all around us. They are a gift to us. When God speaks this way it is awesome, but we can choose to ignore it.

2. When those cells and organs form the human being, we also develop a sense of right and wrong. Everyone everywhere is affected. We know that we fall short. We are sinners. Conscience is a gift by which He speaks in a compelling way but we can choose to ignore it.

3. Beyond looking within we become aware that around us the picture is no better. Something is terribly wrong in the world. Violence, crime, hatred, selfishness, and greed are everywhere. God practically screams at us in the news headlines. Bad things happen and it seems God is speaking of justice. Good things happen to us and we hear Him communicate love and protection. When Jesus appeared on earth He said He came with Good News. When God speaks to us through circumstances it is with a challenging voice, but again we can just ignore it.

4. Alright, says God, I'll put it in writing. Over 95% of the world's population has a substantial, or even complete, translation of the Bible available in its native language. In the Bible God speaks with commanding authority. It rings true, comes true and makes people true in a way no other

book ever has. It's another Christmas gift. But again, we may choose to ignore it.

5. God's final word is embodied in the Person of His crucified Son. It's as though God is calling to us from the cross where Jesus seems to be saying, "This is my final invitation. If you insist on going lost it will have to be over my dead body."

And we have a choice.

NEWS ANYONE?

Angels proclaimed good news of great joy to the shepherds. What was so great about this news? I watched our TV news recently… again! Several times I've felt like not watching the news anymore because it is mostly bad news. Murders, drug deals, overdoses, protests, corruption, war, robberies, accidents, fires, earthquakes and tornadoes are frequent topics. Will there ever be good news? Rarely.

Four lepers outside the besieged and starving city of Samaria back in the 8th century B.C. discovered that the enemies had fled leaving masses of goods and food behind. An ominous noise had frightened them off. The lepers feasted and then said, *"This is a day of good news and we are keeping it to ourselves."* 2 Kings 7:9 They shared the good news and saved the citizens of Samaria from starvation. Centuries later the angels' message to the shepherds at Bethlehem claimed to bring GOOD NEWS too! The reason stated was that we have been given a Savior.

Many people's reaction is, "Savior? We don't need a savior. We're doing just fine the way we are." Others may say, "We'll call if we need you. Otherwise stay out of our lives." Still others respond with, "Savior! Yes, that is what I need."

The starving citizens of Samaria had no problem with acknowledging need. When I watch the news I am repeatedly reminded that the world in general is NOT doing just fine. Furthermore, the question of whether we think we are doing fine depends on the standard or criteria we set. God declares that the most important, and most logical, requirement is to love God with all our heart, mind, soul and strength. The second most important thing is to love others. (Mark 12:30-31) How do we fare on that score? We all need a Savior. *"All have sinned and fall short…" Romans 3:23*

There is a sunny side to all this.

THE INNKEEPER

What was he thinking when Joseph and Mary came to his door?

"Hello, I'm the innkeeper. I see that you are going to read about me again. I want to put in a word first. Preachers have been on my case for 2000 years all over the world. Every year they get after me for putting Mary and Joseph into the stable. You know, if your wife kept reminding you every day for a week about a mistake you made, you would be upset. What about me? This has been going on for 2000 years. Just think of how low my self-esteem is by now."

The innkeeper has a point. For centuries people have questioned what kind of an innkeeper would allow a woman to go to the stable to have her child born. Did he care? Did he have a choice?

Perhaps he was a **helpless** pawn caught in the crush of circumstances? Maybe he had no real choice. He didn't make everybody come. He couldn't provide for everyone. Why are we blaming him if Mary and Joseph had no place left to stay? He had more than enough problems before they even came. The Romans and their demands made life nearly unbearable for the townspeople. The stream of poor people that kept coming for help was more than one innkeeper could handle. He really had too much coming at him. He could hardly cope with day to day life and now he's being called onto the carpet for this too?

Maybe the innkeeper was not stressed out, just a **hardened** man, tossed around by the vicissitudes of life, battered by hard knocks, calloused by the cruelties of those who had taken advantage of him. He had long ago learned not to be vulnerable, not to show concern. To make it in life you had to be tough, when the going gets tough the tough get going. Wimps get trampled. Giving people get ripped off. Show a crack in your emotions and people will worm their way in to drain you of all you've got. Why should he care about this couple pleading for a place to stay? They would just have to tough it out somehow themselves. If they could make a go of it in the stable, fine. If not, too bad. Life never gave him any breaks, and he won't be handing them out to others either.

Perhaps the innkeeper was neither stressed out nor hardened, but just a greedy **hoarding** type. The forced inflow of people due to Caesar's decree was a windfall for him. He was rubbing his hands with glee late into the night each day as hapless souls scoured the town for a place to stay. Each traveler was measured in terms of dollar (or shekel) signs. Every nook in the inn had a price. The value of life came strictly in terms of material gain and he was out to get as much of it for himself as he could. Kindness, caring and generosity had long ago taken flight. Everybody was looking after himself and he was not to be outdone.

Maybe the innkeeper was not all stressed out, nor greedy, nor hardened. Maybe he figured that people are doing OK. The world is getting better and somehow we are going to save ourselves eventually. He was a secular **humanist**. He sounded and looked good. He came across as civilized and caring. He did what he could to find a place for Mary, but to the explanations Joseph gave he said, "So, this child is to be some sort of Messiah? What makes you think this world needs a Messiah? Civilization is developing. We are improving so many things constantly in government, education, medicine, culture agriculture, etc. The great teachers of our time are showing us the way. Mankind is going to elevate itself above much of the negative stuff that is happening now. We are moving toward the utopian society. A Savior Messiah is not needed."

Within a few months the children up to age 2 in that same Bethlehem were massacred. A few years later the religious leaders themselves engineered the crucifixion of the only good man around. By 70 A.D. the Romans had perpetrated one of the cruelest conquests of Jerusalem known, crushing and destroying the people and the temple. So much for utopia.

There is a sense in which each of us is an innkeeper in life. Who we allow to lodge there, the things we make room for and the things we exclude show what we believe in. Perhaps you see yourself reflected in one of the innkeepers conjectured above. Or maybe there is room in your inn for the Lord today.

If we let Him in He'll bring the sunny side along.

KEEP HIM IN THE MANGER

Christmas is over and the decorations are being packed away. Among them may well be a nativity scene with the baby Jesus in a manger, safely stowed away. That is all normal and appropriate. Next year He'll come out again still in the manger. That is also good unless that is the only place we'll ever want Him to be. If, in our heart of hearts we want Him to stay there, we think He'll be no threat to our lifestyle. We can handle a cute baby but not a bold preacher of righteousness. But He did not stay in the manger.

He was heralded as the coming King of the Jews which provoked King Herod to try to kill Him. They escaped to Egypt. As an itinerant preacher of righteousness and truth He earned the resentment of many. When He claimed deity as the Son of God some tried to stone Him to death.

When He offered to be Saviour of the people and free them from the penalty of sin He aroused the jealousy of the religious leaders. Eventually they engineered the crucifixion.

Will we try to keep Him in the manger so that He doesn't interfere with our plans or disturb our lifestyle? The best Christmas will be one in which Jesus is given the place He deserves.

A MESSY CHRISTMAS

Christmas brings thoughts of joy, peace, happiness and lovely scenes. We even picture nativity scenes that are ideals of pleasantness and beauty. But it wasn't like that at all for Joseph and Mary. Think about what they faced:

- A pregnant teen-aged girl trying to convince her parents of her innocence.
- What was it like for her to explain to Joseph before God intervened by sending an angel to confirm the truth.
- Mary would have been the subject of community gossip and accusing looks.
- How about a 145 kilometer trip to Bethlehem from Nazareth on a donkey just before the birth was due? What was it like to arrive in Bethlehem to find no room available but labor pains setting in seriously?

- We've probably heard resentful responses like, "I wasn't born in a barn!" Jesus was. Not much beauty or delight in that.
- How about fleeing to another country not long after the birth because Herod's soldiers had been sent on a baby slaughtering mission to Bethlehem.

Their return to Nazareth didn't stop the slander, it continued into Jesus' thirties during His public ministry. A sword of another kind slashed Mary's heart at the crucifixion, but through it all the angelic message to teen-aged Mary was, "Fear not!" And it did turn out spectacularly well!

"Unto you is born this day a Savior who is Christ the Lord." Luke 2:11

We can celebrate the sunny side of Christmas but it wasn't like that for them.

BELONGING

She just didn't belong here! She was a foreigner, an immigrant from Moab. Some of the Jewish people despised the Moabites because they were descendants of a drunken incest perpetrated by Lot's daughters after escaping Sodom *(see Genesis 19:30-38)*. Her nation was considered by some Jews as an enemy, even though distantly related.

This lady was a desperate young widow, and would be a drain on any resources available. Her mother-in-law had strongly urged her not to come to Bethlehem with her, but to stay in Moab on the other side of the Dead Sea. Her chances of landing a husband in this foreign country would be very low. To survive she would be reduced to gleaning leftover grain during the barley and wheat harvest. The future was looking grim. BUT!!

Ruth's diligence, her love for her mother-in-law Naomi, her humility and her great attitude impressed Boaz, a leading man in Bethlehem. He owned the fields where this woman happened to be gleaning.

Attraction turned to love and then marriage. Their firstborn son was Obed. Their great grandson was King David. And many generations later Joseph and Mary, descendants of David, parented the child Jesus in that same town of Bethlehem. She was a vital link in the coming of the Messiah for us all. Happy Christmas!

She did belong even though her name was Ruth, the Moabitess.

IT WASN'T LIKE THAT

We've become used to nativity pageants or scenes that are beautiful, clean-looking, comfortable and even delightful. That fits nicely into a church sanctuary but it just wasn't like that for Mary and Joseph. A 145 km donkey ride from Nazareth to Bethlehem, when more than eight months pregnant, would hardly be comfortable. Near panic over finding a place to take Mary for the delivery of her child that night in crowded Bethlehem was not a serene experience. A stable, likely a cave being used as a barn, does not compare with a sterile delivery room in the hospital. Having no medical personnel on hand didn't add to Joseph's confidence either. To cap it all off, a late night visit by lowest-class shepherds straight from the field with no hand-sanitizer in sight would hardly add to a disease free state for the event.

But that is the way it was. There was no grand entrance, no jubilant parade and welcoming parties seemed to be restricted to angels and shepherds. The magi came later. If any recognition from Jewish royalty was to come it would be in the form of soldiers sent to kill male babies in order to eliminate competition for the kingship.

But Joseph and Mary put up with it all, escaped the massacre and rejoiced in Jesus' birth.

It takes a lot to stay on the sunny side.

WHY BETHLEHEM?

Why was Bethlehem chosen as the birthplace for Jesus? There were other towns closer to Nazareth. Why wouldn't one of them do? Why not Nazareth itself? If it is going to be somewhere else, why not Jerusalem? Wouldn't this big event get better exposure there? Yet, Micah 5:2 predicted 400 years in advance: *"But you, Bethlehem Ephrathah, though you are small among the clans of Judah out of you will come for me one who will be ruler over Israel, whose origins are from of old, from ancient times."* That is wonderful, but why Bethlehem? Why go there at this late stage in Mary's pregnancy? Would you put your wife on a donkey or donkey cart for a 145 km trip during the last stage of her pregnancy? It must have been an awful journey. I can just imagine weary comments like, "Do we have to go any further? Couldn't we just stay here? Joseph, I can't take it anymore!" There was a Bethlehem in the territory of Zebulon not far from Nazareth. Why not that Bethlehem? It would have been so much easier on Mary. But it had to be in Judah as predicted, convenient substitutes and easier short-cuts were not acceptable.

When the angel announced that the baby Mary was expecting would be the Messiah, you can be sure that the devil heard it too. Can you imagine the consternation among Satan and his fallen angels? A Redeemer was coming into the world! Their number one enemy was on the offensive. How are we going to attack? I can just picture the scheming as the Devil calls together his war cabinet. You see, Satan does scheme. 2 Corinthians 2:11 *"... in order that Satan might not outwit us. For we are not unaware of his schemes."*

I wonder if this is how the Devil's strategy meeting went. "So she's going to have a baby in nine months. Somehow God is going to arrange for them to be in Bethlehem at that time. We'll have to come up with a plan to make life really difficult for Mary and Joseph when they travel to Bethlehem in Judea. That will likely kill the baby and her. Yes, we'll hatch a truly devilish plan." And the demons were rubbing their hands with glee. But it backfired.

Satan has done that kind of thing before. Think of Pharaoh deciding to kill all the male babies just when Moses, their deliverer, was born but Pharaoh ended up raising him in his own palace! Then there's Joseph unjustly confined to an Egyptian prison, but he became Prime Minister and delivered the Israelites from famine. What about Daniel in the lion's den? He was spared but his accusers ended up being eaten. Each time the diabolical plan was turned around and thereby fulfilled God's plan.

This Christmas season, when you hear the story again, think of how the trip to Bethlehem again fulfilled God's plan and foiled Satan's hopes. The Lord can do that in our lives too.

There's victory on the sunny side.

THEME 3

Compassion

What does it mean to have, and express, compassion?

"Be kind and compassionate to one another, forgiving each other,
just as in Christ God forgave you."
Ephesians 4:32

THE BLACK TELEPHONE

When I was a young boy, my father had one of the first telephones in our neighborhood. I remember the polished, old case fastened to the wall. The shiny receiver hung on the side of the box. I was too little to reach the telephone, but used to listen with fascination when my mother talked into it. Then I discovered that somewhere inside the wonderful device lived an amazing person. Her name was "Information Please" and there was nothing she did not know. "Information Please" could supply anyone's number and the correct time.

My personal experience with the genie-in-a-bottle came one day while my mother was visiting a neighbor. Amusing myself at the tool bench in the basement, I whacked my finger with a hammer, the pain was terrible, but there seemed no point in crying because there was no one home to give sympathy. I walked around the house sucking my throbbing finger, finally arriving at the stairway. The telephone! Quickly, I ran for the footstool in the parlor and dragged it to the landing. Climbing up, I unhooked the receiver in the parlor and held it to my ear.

"Information, please," I said into the mouthpiece just above my head. A click or two and a small clear voice spoke into my ear. "Information."

"I hurt my finger..." I wailed into the phone, the tears came readily enough now that I had an audience. "Isn't your mother home?" came the question. "Nobody's home but me," I blubbered. "Are you bleeding?" the voice asked. "No," I replied. "I hit my finger with the hammer and it hurts." "Can you open the icebox?" she asked. I said I could. "Then chip off a little bit of ice and hold it to your finger," said the voice.

After that, I called "Information Please" for everything. I asked her for help with my geography, and she told me where Philadelphia was. She helped me with my math. She told me that my pet chipmunk I had caught in the park just the day before, would eat fruit and nuts. Then, there was the time Petey, our pet canary, died. I called, "Information Please," and told her the sad story. She listened, and then said things grown-ups say to soothe a child. But I was not consoled. I asked her, "Why is it that birds should sing so beautifully and bring joy to all families, only to end up as a heap of feathers on the bottom of a cage?" She must have sensed my deep concern, for she said quietly, "Paul, always remember that there are other worlds to sing in." Somehow I felt better.

Another day I was on the telephone, "Information Please." "Information," said in the now familiar voice. "How do I spell fix?" I asked. All this took place in a small town in the Pacific Northwest. When I was nine years old, we moved across the country to Boston. I missed my friend very much. "Information Please" belonged in that old wooden box back home and I somehow never thought of trying the shiny new phone that sat on the table in the hall. As I grew into my teens, the memories of those childhood conversations never really left me. Often, in moments of doubt and perplexity I would recall the serene sense of security I had then. I appreciated now how patient, understanding, and kind she was to have spent her time on a little boy.

A few years later, on my way west to college, my plane put down in Seattle. I had about a half-hour or so between planes. I spent 15 minutes or so on the phone with my sister, who lived there now. Then without thinking what I was doing, I dialed my hometown operator and said, "Information Please." Miraculously, I heard the small, clear voice I knew so well. "Information." I hadn't planned this, but I heard myself saying, "Could you please tell me how to spell fix?" There was a long pause. Then came the soft spoken answer,

"I guess your finger must have healed by now." I laughed, "So it's really you," I said. "I wonder if you have any idea how much you meant to me during that time?" "I wonder," she said, "if you know how much your call meant to me. I never had any children and I used to look forward to your calls." I told her how often I had thought of her over the years and I asked if I could call her again when I came back to visit my sister. "Please do," she said. "Just ask for Sally."

Three months later I was back in Seattle. A different voice answered, "Information." I asked for Sally. "Are you a friend?" she said. "Yes, a very old friend," I answered. "I'm sorry to have to tell you this," She said. "Sally had been working part time the last few years because she was sick. She died five weeks ago." Before I could hang up, she said, "Wait a minute, did you say your name was Villard?" "Yes." I answered. Well, Sally left a message for you. She wrote it down in case you called. "Let me read it to you." The note said, "Tell him there are other worlds to sing in. He'll know what I mean." I thanked her and hung up. I knew what Sally meant. Never underestimate the impression you may make on others. Whose life have you touched today?

Based on an account by Paul Villard of his own personal experience. It was originally published in the June, 1966 edition of Readers Digest.

GRATITUDE

The owner of a home across the street from John Hopkins Hospital in Baltimore, Maryland, would often rent rooms to out of town patients. They came for treatments or appointments and needed an over-night stay. Late one afternoon the owner answered the door to find a startling sight. The physical condition of the man almost caused the owner to shut the door. "*His small body was stooped and shrivelled and his face was red, raw and lopsided from swelling. His voice was pleasant as he asked for a room for the night."*

In a voice that was pleasantly different from his appearance the man explained that he was scheduled for treatments at the hospital but needed a place to sleep. He had spent all afternoon trying to find a place but had been turned away repeatedly. When the owner hesitated the man offered to sleep in the rocking chair on the porch. The owner felt a bit ashamed and told him they had a bed for him and invited him to join them for supper.

Conversation that evening revealed that he was a fisherman, trying to support himself, his daughter and a crippled son-in-law plus five grandchildren. The owner's children delighted to hear his stories and were not turned off by his appearance. Instead, his attitude of gratitude in spite of serious troubles was inspiring. Before leaving them he asked if he could stay with them during future appointments. He said he felt at home here. They readily agreed, though neighbors criticized them for harboring that awful looking man.

Every time the man came back he brought some seafood. They looked forward to the visits, which soon ended due to successful treatments. They missed him and were glad that they hadn't judged him by appearances.

LOCKED DOOR

A compassionate doctor decided to help one of his patients by providing her with the rent for her apartment. She was battling poverty and fearful of eviction by the landlord. In her despair she had confided in the doctor who had asked her why she seemed so stressed out. With the rent money in his pocket he came to the door and knocked. No answer. He continued knocking several times because he heard some commotion inside the apartment. He tried to open the door but it was locked. Eventually he gave up and went back home.

A few days later he met the lady on the street and told her about his attempted visit. "Oh no," she exclaimed, "I thought it was the landlord coming to collect the rent."

Could it be that some who are reading this are like that lady? They have locked the door against a compassionate Savior who comes offering an amazing gift. Feeling that the Visitor is just coming to condemn or intrude upon the reader's lifestyle, the door is locked.

Jesus said, *"Here I am! I stand at the door and knock. If anyone hears my voice and opens the door, I will come in..." Revelations 3:20*

MAXIMILIAN KOLBE

A Franciscan priest, Maximilian Kolbe, was imprisoned in Auschwitz by the Nazis in February of 1941. Rather than allowing his circumstances to get him down, he looked for how he could serve others. He shared his meagre food, gave up his bunk to prisoners who did not get a bed, prayed for the guards and generally sought to be a positive influence. He was known as the Saint of Auschwitz.

In July of that year one prisoner escaped. It was the practise of the Nazis to randomly place 10 other prisoners in solitary confinement and let them starve to death if a prisoner escaped. This was to discourage any other attempts to escape. Franciszek Gajowniczek was one of the ones selected to die by starvation. He immediately despaired of ever seeing his wife and children again. He pleaded for mercy. No exceptions! At this the priest offered to take the man's place. He had no family and was already old. This huge offer was accepted by the warden. In confinement Maximilian sang with the other 9, taught them the ways of the Lord and told them to anticipate a better future after death. Death row seemed to be turned into a haven. Maximilian was the last to die, but not of starvation. They finally injected carbolic acid to bring on death.

After the war was over Gajowniczek devoted the rest of his life to honoring this priest and the Lord. "Somebody died for me," he declared, "similar to Christ dying for our sins."

Likely none of us has had to endure circumstances anywhere close to those of Maximilian, yet he was able to live on the sunny side.

BUT I MEANT WELL!

Have you ever said something that conveyed a second meaning very different from what you intended? Was it embarrassing? Were you able to rescue yourself?

A business man found it necessary to travel to other cities several times a year because of the nature of his business. On one short trip he decided to drive home rather than stay another night in the motel as had been planned. During the last hour before arriving at home a thunderstorm broke out. The driving rain, the flashes of lightning and the peals of thunder made it more difficult but he arrived home safely after midnight. Since the family was not expecting him yet, he decided to tiptoe softly to the bedroom. Just as he reached the slightly ajar bedroom door, a flash of lightening allowed him to see that his two young daughters were in the bed with his wife. Not willing to awaken them he retreated to the living room and settled down on the couch.

In the morning the surprised family was delighted to see him but sad that he had missed out on a good sleep. He told the girls that he understood why they went to where mommy was. It was a scary night. But he expressed the hope that they would soon become brave enough to cope on their own.

The next trip was by airplane, and the family was waiting for him in the airport for his arrival home. As soon as the seven year old daughter saw him she ran to him and shouted, "Daddy, daddy! I have good news." Even the crowd paused to listen to this girl's exciting news. "What is it, dear," asked the dad. The girl declared, "No one slept with mommy while you were away."

Some laughed, others tried to stifle a chuckle. The mother turned red with embarrassment and the father was stunned to silence. Having no clue as to why people were reacting like that the girl was on the verge of tears. A wise man stepped up to her and said, "Little girl, do you mean that you were brave enough to stay in your own bed even if you were scared of the dark? You are a very special girl." The girl did not need correction, just affirmation of her good intentions.

The crowd applauded and cheered. His presence of mind rescued the girl. It takes a special insight to know what to say to a person who meant well, but didn't realize what the other implications were.

ACTS OF KINDNESS

I was at the corner grocery store buying some early potatoes. I noticed a small boy, delicate of bone and feature, ragged but clean, hungrily apprising a basket of freshly picked green peas. I paid for my potatoes but was also drawn to the display of fresh green peas. I am a pushover for creamed peas and new potatoes. Pondering the peas, I couldn't help overhearing the conversation between Mr. Miller (the store owner) and the ragged boy next to me.

'Hello Barry, how are you today?' ;

'H'lo, Mr. Miller. Fine, thank ya. Jus' admirin' them peas. They sure look good'

'They are good, Barry. How's your Ma?'

'Fine. Gittin' stronger alla' time.'

'Good. Anything I can help you with?'

'No, Sir. Jus' admirin' them peas.'

'Would you like to take some home?' asked Mr. Miller.

'No, Sir. Got nuthin' to pay for 'em with.'

'Well, what have you to trade me for some of those peas?'

'All I got's my prize marble here.'

'Is that right? Let me see it', said Miller.

'Here 'tis. She's a dandy.'

'I can see that. Hmm mmm, only thing is this one is blue and I sort of go for red. Do you have a red one like this at home?' the store owner asked.

'Not zackley but almost.'

'Tell you what. Take this sack of peas home with you and next trip this way let me look at that red marble'. Mr. Miller told the boy. 'Sure will. Thanks Mr. Miller.'

Mrs. Miller, who had been standing nearby, came over to help me. With a smile she said, 'There are two other boys like him in our community, all three are in very poor circumstances. Jim just loves to bargain with them for peas, apples, tomatoes, or whatever. When they come back with their red marbles, and they always do, he decides he doesn't like red after all and he sends them home with a bag of produce for a green marble or an orange one, when they come on their next trip to the store.' I left the store smiling to myself, impressed with this man. A short time later I moved to Colorado, but I never forgot the story of this man, the boys, and their bartering for marbles.

Several years went by, each more rapidly than the previous one. Just recently I had occasion to visit some old friends in that Idaho community and while I was there learned that Mr. Miller had died. They were having his visitation that evening and knowing my friends wanted to go, I agreed to accompany them. Upon arrival at the mortuary we fell into line to meet the relatives of the deceased and to offer whatever words of comfort we could. Ahead of us in line were three young men. One was in an army uniform and the other two wore nice haircuts, dark suits and white shirts, all very professional looking. They approached Mrs. Miller, standing composed and smiling by her husband's casket.

Each of the young men hugged her, kissed her on the cheek, spoke briefly with her and moved on to the casket. Her misty light blue eyes followed them as, one by one; each young man stopped briefly and placed his own warm hand over the cold pale hand in the casket. Each left the mortuary awkwardly, wiping his eyes. Our turn came to meet Mrs. Miller I told her who I was and reminded her of the story from those many years ago and what she had told me about her husband's bartering for marbles. With her eyes glistening, she took my hand and led me to the casket.

"Those three young men who just left were the boys I told you about. They just told me how they appreciated the things Jim 'traded' them. Now, at last, when Jim could not change his mind about color or size, they came to pay their debt.

We've never had a great deal of the wealth of this world," she confided, "but right now, Jim would consider himself the richest man in Idaho." ;

With loving gentleness she lifted the lifeless fingers of her deceased husband. Resting underneath were three exquisitely shined red marbles.

We will not be remembered by our words, but by our kind deeds. Life is not measured by the breaths we take, but by the moments that take our breath away.

W.E. Peterson, October 1975, Ensign magazine

NOTICED

The king of England agreed to attend the laying of a cornerstone for a new hospital in a city he had rarely or maybe never visited. As a result huge crowds assembled on the day of his arrival. Thousands thronged the streets and converged upon the grounds where the stone was to be laid. A very large choir of school children were scheduled to sing for the king. When the whole ceremony was over and the king left for his palace a teacher noticed one girl in the choir dissolve into tears. "What's wrong, little girl," asked the teacher. "Didn't you see the king?" "Yes, I did," sobbed the girl, "but he didn't see me."

It's true that the girl's expectation was unrealistic, but we all experience times when we wish we would be noticed. It's discouraging to be ignored. That's when the promise in Psalm 33:18 is encouraging. *"The eyes of the Lord are on those who fear him, on those whose hope is in his unfailing love."*

In a world of nearly seven billion people on a planet that is almost an invisible speck in a vast universe it is absolutely remarkable that God notices every individual.

PERSISTENT LOVE

Jennifer Wright was born in an Ohio hospital on July 17, 1972. Even though she was a bit premature all seven pounds of her seemed to be in great shape. However, at three months the mother noticed swelling in her right foot. The doctors couldn't figure out what caused it even after the swelling spread to her right leg, right hand and part of her buttocks. After nearly three years of frustrating searches the Children's Hospital in Denver, CO identified it as the rare Parkes-Weber syndrome. Lymphatic valves in her leg were missing, preventing the upward flow of fluids. Fluids simply piled up lower down. Unless corrected the fluid would become stale and infected, resulting in amputation.

Teasing, bullying, special clothes and made-to-fit shoes plus many other inconveniences and embarrassments made life difficult for her. Grandfather Edward Wright was extremely distressed over the deteriorating situation. Already having seven patented inventions to his name he was determined to create something that would help Jennifer. Experimental therapy using a synthetic sleeve hadn't worked. Then he made a bold statement. "With the Lord's help, before I die, I'm going to do something for my granddaughter." He worked on his plan many long hours, often well into the night. On Nov. 15, 1980 the doctor tested the invention on his own arm and immediately chose to use it on Jennifer. It consisted of a three-part, electronically pressure-controlled sleeve. There were dramatic results right away. Grandpa Wright became legally blind two months after completing the invention, but Jennifer made sure that each step of progress was joyfully shared with the grandfather. Jennifer and her grandpa developed a very special bond of love. Within a year Jennifer was nearly normal and only needed the pump one hour a day. Soon his device was being use in several countries around the world. In Feb., 1986, Edward Wright received the Inventor of the Year award from the Patent Law Association of Pittsburg. But his biggest achievement was persistent love.

Based on a Ladies' Home Journal article by Patrick Pacheco, Oct., 1985 and summarized in the Apr., 1986 Readers' Digest

Love conquers all!

A ROSE

Amanda McBroom, the writer of the song, *The Rose,* must have experienced great discouragement and despair in her life, or else observed it in someone dear to her. The third verse of the song expresses it this way.

> *When the night has been so lonely and the road has been too long,*
> *And you think that love is only for the lucky and the strong,*
> *Just remember in the winter far beneath the bitter snows*
> *Lies the seed that, with the sun's love, in the spring becomes*
> *the rose.*

Some of us may be identifying with the dark and lonely night right now. Currently, life's journey is a tough one for some of you. It may be that you are haunted by things done wrong or circumstances gone wrong. There seems to be no way out. But there is hope. There are people who care about you and God cares about you too. He is able to see you through.

There's hope on the sunny side.

TEDDY

Elizabeth Ballard had a heart for students who were in difficult situations. In 1974 she submitted a story to *Home Life* magazine, a Baptist family publication, where it was clearly labeled as fiction, but the content was touchingly true to life. Some of the incidents in the story were modeled after her own experiences or those of others.

Her story was about a fictional elementary teacher, Mrs. Thompson, who wanted to care about all her students the same but there in the front row, slumped in his seat, was a little boy named Teddy

Stoddard (in some versions Stallard). He didn't play well with the other children, his clothes were messy and he constantly needed a bath. And Teddy could be unpleasant. At times she resented him.

When she reviewed his file she was surprised to discover the following. Teddy's first grade teacher wrote, "Teddy is a bright child with a ready laugh. He does his work neatly and has good manners...he is a joy to be around." His second grade teacher wrote, "Teddy is an excellent student, well-liked by his classmates, but he is troubled because his mother has a terminal illness and life at home must be a struggle." His third grade teacher wrote, "His mother's death has been hard on him. He tries to do his best but his father doesn't show much interest and his home life will soon affect him if some steps aren't taken." Teddy's fourth grade teacher wrote, "Teddy is withdrawn and doesn't show much interest in school. He doesn't have many friends and sometimes sleeps in class."

By now, Mrs. Thompson realized the problem and she was ashamed of herself. She felt even worse when her students brought her Christmas presents, wrapped in beautiful ribbons and bright paper, except for Teddy's. His present was clumsily wrapped in the heavy, brown paper that he got from a grocery bag. Mrs. Thompson took pains to open it in the middle of the other presents. Some of the children started to laugh when she found a rhinestone bracelet with some of the stones missing and a bottle that was one quarter full of perfume. But she stifled the children's laughter when she exclaimed how pretty the bracelet was, putting it on, and dabbing some of the perfume on her wrist.

Teddy Stoddard stayed after school that day just long enough to say, "Mrs. Thompson, today you smelled just like my Mom used to." After the children left she cried for at least an hour. On that very day, she quit teaching reading, and writing, and arithmetic. Instead, she began to teach children. Mrs. Thompson paid particular attention to Teddy. As she worked with him, his mind seemed to come alive. The more she encouraged him, the faster he responded. By the end of the year, Teddy had become one of the smartest children in the class and, despite her lie that she would love all the children the same, Teddy became one of her "teacher's pets." A year later, she found a note under her door, from Teddy, telling her that she was still the best teacher he ever had in his whole life. Six years went by before she got another note from Teddy. He then wrote that he had finished high school, third in his class, and she was still the best teacher he ever had in his whole life.

Four years after that, she got another letter, saying that while things had been tough at times, he'd stayed in school, had stuck with it, and would soon graduate from college with the highest of honors. He assured Mrs. Thompson that she was still the best and favorite teacher he ever had in his whole life.

Then four more years passed and yet another letter came. This time he explained that after he got his bachelor's degree, he decided to go a little further. The letter explained that she was still the best teacher he ever had. But now his name was a little longer. The letter was signed, Theodore F. Stoddard, M.D.

The story doesn't end there. You see, there was yet another letter that spring. Teddy said he'd met this girl and was going to be married. He explained that his father had died a couple of years ago and he was wondering if Mrs. Thompson might agree to sit in the place at the wedding that was usually reserved for the mother of the groom.

Of course, Mrs. Thompson did. And guess what? She wore that bracelet, the one with several rhinestones missing. And she made sure she was wearing the perfume that Teddy remembered his mother wearing on their last Christmas together.

They hugged each other, and Dr. Stoddard whispered in Mrs. Thompson's ear, "Thank you, Mrs. Thompson, for believing in me.

Thank you so much for making me feel important and showing me that I could make a difference."

Mrs. Thompson, with tears in her eyes, whispered back. She said, "Teddy, you have it all wrong. You were the one who taught me that I could make a difference. I didn't know how to teach until I met you.

Even though this touching tale is an invention, there may well be someone in our life who could be rescued from a life of despair by our compassion and care. Elizabeth Ballard of North Carolina has expressed disappointment that her fictional work continues to be circulated as a true story. However, perhaps we can make it a true story for someone else. That would truly bring in the sunshine!

THE WOODEN BOWL

A frail old man went to live with his son, daughter-in-law, and four-year- old grandson. The old man's hands trembled, his eyesight was blurred, and his step faltered. The family ate together at the table. But the elderly grandfather's shaky hands and failing sight made eating difficult. Peas rolled off his spoon onto the floor. When he grasped the glass, milk spilled on the tablecloth.

The son and daughter-in-law became irritated with the mess. "We must do something about father," said the son. "I've had enough of his spilled milk, noisy eating, and food on the floor."

So the husband and wife set a small table in the corner. There, Grandfather ate alone while the rest of the family enjoyed dinner. Since Grandfather had broken a dish or two, his food was served in a wooden bowl. When the family glanced in Grandfather's direction, sometimes he had a tear in his eye as he sat alone. Still, the only words the couple had for him were sharp admonitions when he dropped a fork or spilled food.

The four-year-old watched it all in silence. One evening before supper, the father noticed his son playing with wood scraps on the floor. He asked the child sweetly, "What are you making?" Just as sweetly, the boy responded, "Oh, I am making a little bowl for you and mama to eat your food in when I grow up." The four-year-old smiled and went back to work.

The words so struck the parents that they were speechless. Then tears started to stream down their cheeks. Though no word was spoken, both knew what must be done. That evening the husband took Grandfather's hand and gently led him back to the family table. For the remainder of his days he ate every meal with the family. And for some reason, neither husband nor wife seemed to care any longer when a fork was dropped, milk spilled, or the tablecloth soiled.

A GREAT FATHER'S DAY

His son had left home while still in his teens. After eighteen years that son found himself reduced to begging for change from people on the street. Circumstances had left him homeless in Philadelphia, and destitute for the last year. He tapped a pedestrian on the shoulder and asked for a dime. Upon turning around the pedestrian found himself facing his son. He had come looking for him, undoubtedly asking the Lord to lead him in his search. What an unbelievable answer to his prayer. The young man received much more than a dime. Reconciliation, a home and eventually a respectable life all came his way.

So often people keep pounding the futile pavement in search of happiness that just won't come. Our heavenly Father is searching too. But He is searching for prodigals willing to come home.

REAL SPORTSMANSHIP

Sara Tucholsky was a member of the Western Oregon Wolves baseball team, but that was often as far as it got. Her batting ability was so low that she seldom got to play. On this Saturday in April, 2008, she was on the roster only because the right outfielder had been pulled. It was a decisive game. The winner would qualify for the division finals. The loser would be done.

It was her turn at bat. She had never, ever, hit a home run but on that day she connected. The ball sailed over the left-field fence for a home run. With two runners on base, the three runs would be a crucial score. In Sara's excitement she rounded first base without touching the bag. The coach called her back to first base but in her eager turn-around something popped in her knee. She collapsed in agony. She couldn't even stand up, much less run the bases to home. If anyone on her team helped her she would be disqualified. What could be done?

While the umpires discussed this unusual development, the Central Washington University team's first base player made a suggestion to the umpires. What if she were to help Sara make it around the bases? Together with the short stop player the two girls carried Sara around the bases making sure that they lowered her at each base to touch the bag. The spectators rose to their feet and cheered wildly. It was an outstanding demonstration of sportsmanship surpassing even Valentine's Day love.

Source: Max Lucado, Unshakable Hope, pp. 71-78

THEME 4

Creation

How did we and everything around us get here?
Why is there something instead of nothing?

"You alone are the LORD. You made the heavens, even the highest heavens, and all their starry host, the earth and all that is on it, the seas and all that is in them. You give life to everything, and the multitudes of heaven worship you." Nehemiah 9:6

THE BOTANIST

A botanist wandered into the mountains of Scotland to look for some of his favorite flowers. He spotted one that was very small but very beautiful under the microscope. Setting his microscope up in such a way as to gain the maximum benefit from the sun he spent a long time looking at it from various angles. So focused was he on his observations that he did not notice the tall, weather-beaten shepherd approaching. When the shepherd's shadow fell across his microscope, he looked up and noticed a somewhat bemused man watching him. "What are you doing with such a common thing as a tiny flower?" he asked. "That's just a waste of time." Without a word the botanist beckoned him to have a look. After a while the shepherd got up and looked at the botanist in a different way. He even had tears in his eyes. "What's the matter?" asked the botanist. "Isn't it beautiful?" The shepherd could hardly speak. "It's more than beautiful, and here I have stepped on many of them without a thought. I thought they were worthless. Mine was the waste."

We may have similarly been very casual about the reason why Jesus came to earth. *"For the Son of Man has come to seek and to save that which was lost." Luke 19:10* We could come to the conclusion that mankind is not worth redeeming, especially not at the cost of death on a cross. But He did it because He loved us and considered us precious. He really cares about you!

There's love on the sunny side.

DUCTUS ARTERIOSUS

What in the world is that??

In his book, *Soul Survivor,* page 69, Philip Yancy writes about his interview with Dr. Paul Brand where the doctor describes a remarkable, crucial and timely event at the birth of a baby. When a fetus is developing, a bypass vessel called the *ductus arteriosus* routes blood around the lungs because there is yet no breathing. The blood, oxygenated via the mother's placenta, goes directly to the developing fetus. At birth, blood must now pass through the lungs to receive oxygen because the baby is now being separated from the mother and breathing air on its own. This shocking experience of the first breath in the lungs, and the first rush of much of the blood through the lungs, must be what causes the baby's first wail. In a day or two (not always in seconds as Dr. Brand thought), a flap completes its descent like a curtain, deflecting all the blood flow. A muscle constricts the ductus arteriosus, which then gradually dissolves. Without this critically timed adjustment, the baby could never survive outside the womb.

How did that life-saving arrangement ever develop? Is it even remotely reasonable to mark it down to blind chance or to mutations which are mistakes, omissions or inversions in the DNA code? Do we ever attribute the invention of any of the multitude of devices, machines or instruments we use to just happening by chance or random mistakes? No, we honor the inventor! We have a very, very highly intelligent Creator to credit with this astounding process and the many other natural marvels that exist.

Thanks from a birth survivor!

EAGLES

Most of us have watched an eagle soaring almost effortlessly across the sky. We may even have been fortunate enough to see one snatch a meal from the river. Where did that eagle get this ability?

Eagles are uniquely designed to maximize their mastery of the skies. Although they have about 7000 feathers the total weight of these feathers is only 600-700 grams (20 ounces). Body temperature can be modified by regulating the position of the feathers. A layer of down keeps them warm when needed. Their bones are hollow but strong and weigh not much more than 250 grams (ten ounces). Wings may extend up to four feet on either side with tapered wing tip feathers that reduce turbulence. Flight speeds can reach 70 km/hr, with a dive clocking in at up to 160 km/hr. The eyesight of an eagle is four to five times sharper than ours, enabling it to see an ant on the ground from the tenth floor. The largest bird nest ever built belonged to an eagle. It was nearly six meters deep and three meters wide.

All of the foregoing adds up to a mighty arsenal of skills. What an amazing design by a very powerful and highly intelligent Designer. Many are the wonders our Creator has provided.

It is fitting to be in awe.

EARS

Did you hear that? What's that rustling in the bushes? Is that a warbler in the distance? A plane taking off and then a jackhammer drown out other sounds. You slap the side of your head as the drone of a mosquito attracts your attention. Home from your walk, Beethoven's 6th Symphony lulls you to sleep on the recliner. All these experiences may be very familiar but we have hardly a clue about what is really going on when we hear sounds. Air vibrations are detected, converted into hydro-dynamic vibrations and then into electrical impulses that reach the brain which evaluates and identifies what it hears. Amazing! How does that work? The level of technology involved is beyond what science has attained or in some aspects hasn't even understood. Let's take a peek at a few of the intricacies.

The outer ear on each side of our head captures the sound waves in the uniquely shaped grooves that funnel them into the ear canal along two paths, a shorter one directly to the canal and a longer path around the outer edge. That seems trivial but the net result is a cleverly designed, tiny split second difference in arrival and intensity at the ear drum on each side. From this the brain calculates the direction and approximate distance from which the sound comes. The two 'sources' on each side effectively create four ears. Wow!

In the middle ear area the drum vibrates and transfers air vibration energy to liquid vibrations. These liquid vibrations reach the three tiniest bones in the human body: hammer, anvil and stirrup. Together these weigh only ten milligrams. Vibrational transfer from air to liquid usually means huge losses due to reflection or bounce at the surface. The energy level is already very small. But the middle ear has been created in such a way that there is nearly zero loss. The ear drum and middle ear bones exactly match the sound wave impedance. The oval window through which the waves travel is about 1/20 the size of the drum, concentrating the sound. The three bones further triple the amplification directed to the inner ear. And it gets even more complex.

In the inner ear the vibrations are changed into electrical neural impulses that travel to about 12,000 miniscule hair-like sensory cells lined up like piano keys. A piano has 88 keys. This apparatus has 12,000! It is not yet understood how this works. From there the auditory nerve transmits the message to the brain for interpretation, which is another wonder!!

In summary, our larynx is built to produce sounds, our mouth and throat modulate them into usable vowels and consonants, and our brain controls and interprets the meaning of sounds that our ears have heard. *Psalm 94:9 states, "Does He who implanted the ear not hear?"* The Lord is very interested in hearing from each one of us, but even more interested in us listening to Him.

There is much more detail in Dr. Werner Gitt's book, The Wonder of Man, to whom I am indebted for this information.

ENDOCRINE SYSTEM

A very essential control feature in our body is the endocrine system. It is a communication network that uses chemical messengers called hormones, reaching every cell by way of the blood stream. The pituitary, thyroid, pancreas, thymus, hypothalamus, adrenal, ovaries and testes glands are part of this system. The hormones maintain a livable level of salt, water and sugar in our body. They initiate and control many bodily functions. They produce physical growth and sexual maturation and have a lot to do with powerful emotions like anger, joy and despair.

Without these controls and communication paths of the nervous and endocrine systems, the human body could not function. There has to be an effective way of coordinating all the various parts of the body so that they function in harmony. Each part has to grow into its function at a compatible rate and do what is needed at just the right time and place. Many of us know from first-hand experience what it takes to organize an event or oversee a team of workers. It definitely cannot be left to chance.

I know very little about the physiology of the human body but I do know that such a complex, intricate, fine-tuned mechanism came by design, not chance. Praise the Lord!

EPIGLOTTIS

Have you ever had food go down the windpipe instead of the esophagus? You probably tried to talk with food in your mouth, or were eating too fast, or tried to swallow too much at a time. That problem will make you very uncomfortable. It can even be life-threatening. I know that from experience.

Did you know that a leaf-like flap of cartilage, just behind the tongue and before the larynx, acts like a policeman directing traffic? When you start to swallow it quickly flaps down to close the lid on the windpipe while the larynx moves up against the lid to keep food from getting into your lungs. That is the job it does all your life, every day, all day and night. Without it you would likely die soon but this little lifesaver hardly ever gets any credit. Not only that, it had to be there right from the start. You can't wait around for thousands or millions of years for it to show up by chance and natural selection as in evolution. It had to be in just the right place with just the right mechanisms and nerves to do the job on day one.

Seeing to such crucial details is the work of a Designer. I am thankful for that.

It's great to be on the sunny side.

EVENING PRIMROSE

The evening primrose is a very unique flowering plant producing a tight rosette of flowers the first year, but the flowers are located spirally on a stem the second year. It produces flowers from late spring to late summer. The flowers are hermaphrodite, meaning that they open visibly fast in the evening and only last until noon the following day. The flower has a bright nectar guide pattern visible to the pollinators like moths, butterflies and bees but we have to use ultraviolet light to see the guide. The seed capsule bursts into four sections at maturity, providing food for the birds and seeds for the next generation of evening primroses. What delightfully interesting features!!

Perhaps the Lord really enjoyed designing that one.

THE EYELIDS

When Dueteronomy 32:10 promises that God will guard us as the *"apple of His eye"* we would be wise to ask ourselves how that is done. In so doing we find that eyelids are able to guard, protect and care for the well-being of the eye. The eyelid consists of skin and muscle that provide the following care for our eyes.

Eyelids blink regularly during waking hours to keep the conjunctiva and cornea moist. Without that it would dry up and become useless. Our soul needs regular care too.

Eyelids close automatically if an object threatens to touch the eye. The eyelids have eyelashes that help to keep some dust and tiny particles away. The seventh cranial nerve can quickly close the eyelids and the third cranial nerve opens them. Our spiritual life is also constantly the target of attack.

Eyelids spread a cleansing, lubricating and disinfecting liquid over the eye to keep it from being contaminated. The Meibomian glands provide the fluids for this, including tears. A duct at the interior corner of the eye can carry excess or used fluid into the nasal cavity which is why we often have to blow our noses when crying. Regular cleansing from wrong is vital.

Eyelids shield the eye from strong lights by covering it, allowing us to sleep better.

All of this is connected to, coordinated with and controlled by the brain. Every aspect has to work harmoniously with the rest of the body. Eyelids are a small but an amazing part of our Creator's work. They did not come about by accident. They teach us that we also need to guard, clean and care for our spiritual life.

Thank you, Lord, for eyelids!

HANDS

The human hand is an astoundingly complex and amazingly versatile part of our body. Nearly a decade was devoted to developing an artificial hand to replicate even a few of the things the human hand can do. Robotics engineers, research scientists and design specialists undertook the Autonomous Robotic Manipulation project in cooperation with the Defense Advanced Research Projects Agency, Harvard University and Yale University. They discovered that "… *creating robot hands with even a fraction of human capabilities has proved an elusive goal."* The amazing dexterity and sensitivity of the human hand is a marvel. More than thirty muscles and thousands of nerve endings manipulate twenty-nine flexible joints. With those it can play a piano, read Braille and thread a needle. They sense hot and cold, smooth and rough, strength of grip or gentleness of touch and more. We really learn to appreciate what our hands can do when we lose the ability to use them. All of our lives they have responded instantly to a vast myriad of tasks we expect of them. How can we possibly entertain even the thought that they developed by chance and natural selection as evolutionists claim? Skilled scientists used years of work and huge sums of money to accomplish a fraction of what the hand can do. None of what they did came by itself. Therefore it stands to reason that hands are the product of a Master Designer who says: *"We are fearfully and wonderfully made."* *Psalm 139:14* We will be held accountable for what we do with them.

Based on CREATION magazine, Vol. 38, #1 2016,
back cover article by David Catchpoole.

NERVES ARE MESSENGERS

How does the brain control the work and reactions of muscles and organs? Our brain is an amazingly complex, super-super 'computer' that looks like a three pound spongy walnut. It sends its commands via a massive network of nerves, reaching every part of our body. The sole of our foot is very sensitive but is equipped to develop a calloused surface if we go barefoot a lot. The eye is the most sensitive part of our body, about 3000 times as sensitive as the foot. The tiniest speck will cause serious irritations. It will never develop a calloused surface to protect itself and for good reasons. Some organs do not depend on volitional messages but operate automatically like the heart and lungs. Again for very good reasons. Most movements of our limbs require conscious decisions, very appropriate. Some messages need instant attention as shown in the statement below.

Of the many nerves in the human body, only the twelve cranial nerves by pass the spinal cord with a hotline to the brain. Flick a finger at my eye and I blink. Chew gum while talking and your tongue darts perilously in and out of chomping molars to steer the gum...all the while snaking from teeth to roof of mouth to lips to teeth again, forming syllables of sound. These speedy movements, guided by sensory input, are made possible by the cranial nerves' short, direct path to the brain.

Four of these cranial nerves deal with vision. The ones controlling eye movement are especially unique. Three of these nerves control eyeball movements (the largest, the optical nerve, carries digitized images from the retina to the brain). Coordinating six tiny muscles, they furnish an advanced tracking system that allows us to lock in, say, on a goldfinch and follow its erratic, dipping flight across the horizon. The same nerves govern the miniscule jerks and glides required by the act of reading... They get the greatest workout of any, moving about 100,000 times each day (equivalent to leg muscles walking 80 kilometers).

The Gift of Pain by Phillip Yancy and Dr. Paul Brand, p.43 – 45

So how does the brain control all this and more? It uses a vast, complex array of nerves to transmit orders to the muscles and organs. It is no stretch to recognize that we are indeed wonderfully made.

PEACOCK SPIDERS

The Peacock Spider of Australia is only about ¼ inch in size but displays a fantastic, colorful design. It is hardly the horrible, detestable image most people connect with spiders. In the words of Michael Eggleton *"...its abdomen is covered by a dense layer of intricately designed scales, similar to those on some butterflies..."* Some colors like red and yellow are produced by pigments, *"...but the iridescent blue is a structural color..."* The tiny patterns of the scales affect the color based on the angle of the observer and the direction from which the light comes.

Why would beauty be invested in such a tiny creature? There is no evolutionary explanation because these colors would do the opposite of giving it a survival advantage. It would be making itself noticeable, not camouflaged. Added beauty does not fit into the scheme of chance mutations for natural selection. Rather, it points to a Creator who just loves to make beautiful things.

We are the benefactors of creative beauty in so many ways.

Based on Creation magazine article, Vol.39, No. 3, 2017

PEANUTS

Apparently George W. Carver, the research scientist, is reputed to have had (or imagined) a conversation with the Lord in which he asked Him, "What is the universe?" It seems that the answer he got was, "George, that's too big for your little head. Suppose you let me take care of the universe."

Greatly humbled, Carver revised his question, "Lord, if the universe is too big for me to understand, tell me: What is a peanut?" The answer was, "Now, George, you've got something your own size. Go to work on the peanut."

Imaginary or not, what was for real is that Carver revolutionized southern agriculture by finding uses for the peanut. Instead of constant soil depletion by repeated crops of cotton, peanuts were grown to enrich the soil. Peanuts became a main crop in many areas. Carver showed how peanuts can be used to make cheese, milk, butter, flour, ink, dyes, soap, stains and even insulating boards. It's absolutely amazing to see the potential our Creator has built into plants.

Little can become much when God is in it.

WHODUNNIT??

Divers off the coast of Japan discovered a circular structure sculpted in the seafloor sand. D. Catchpoole states that this was made up of *"multiple ridges symmetrically radiating out from a small patterned circle in the centre"*. It was like an underwater crop circle we've heard about before. Whodunnit?? More than ten years after this discovery in 1995, they found the culprit. It was a five inch pufferfish. For just over a week the male pufferfish would build this geometric marvel to attract a mate to its nest. The radially aligned peaks and valleys of the outer wall funneled fine sand into the center, just right for the female to place her eggs. No accident. The ability to do this was built in to the DNA of the male by design. It is just one of the many, many marvels in creation.

It's amazing on the sunny side!

Based on Creation magazine article, Vol. 40, p.21

THE EYES OF A REINDEER

The eyes of Arctic reindeer are golden-colored during the long summer and turn a deep blue in winter. David Catchpoole reports that for about twelve years a group of neuroscientists tried to discover why this dramatic change takes place each year. What they found had to do with the reflective surface behind the retina, commonly known as 'cat's eye'. In the bright summer, where they have nearly twenty-four hours of light on some days, that reflective surface is golden so that most of the light is reflected back through the retina. In winter when darkness rules the blue is needed to pick up the shorter wavelengths prominent in situations with less light. Colder weather causes contractions, reducing the spacing between the collagen fibres in the reflective surface which results in picking up the blue wavelengths from the electromagnetic spectrum. This increases the reindeer's ability to see in the darkness.

What a wonderful design feature our Creator has placed in those deer. It is fitting to marvel at such incredible genius and give Him credit for it.

Seems like there's a sunny side to winter too.

Creation magazine article, Vol.39, No. 3, 2017

SEEDS

Many of us have planted seeds in a garden. Some of us may have looked at the seeds in our hand and wondered how this shriveled up little piece can possibly grow into a beautiful flower or a watermelon or a carrot. The powerful genetic programming inside the seed is just waiting for the right conditions of moisture, warmth and nutrients to become what it was meant to be. What amazing potential in such an unpromising item!

We take it all for granted. We simply accept that each seed will consistently produce what we expect from it. We have faith in the solid predictability of what will grow even though placing a tiny bit of "stuff" in the dirt carries little visible promise. We expect beneficial results. But there are enemies. Diseases, insects and hungry animals can ruin our work. We may even trample it ourselves.

The same pattern exists in our relationship to God, the Creator of this marvel. Our tiny seed of faith may seem so powerless and insignificant but God promises huge benefits. However, there are also enemies. Temptations and tests from around us, plus tendencies toward wrong from within us, war against these benefits. Repentance and faith bring forgiveness of sin. Continuing to exercise faith in

God develops character and maturity. The promise of God is that *"anyone who is in Christ is a new person." 2 Corinthians 5:17*

God loves you and is very interested in providing the conditions of spiritual warmth and nutrition that will produce the beneficial and beautiful person you were meant to be.

A SPECK IN SPACE

Most of us have looked up at the night sky and marveled at the sight. What we see, however, is a very small part of what is out there. The Hubble Space Telescope has identified many, many more stars, planets and galaxies without any sign of reaching the end. When it focused on planet Earth we were just a miniscule, blue speck in the vast sea of space.

How could God consider us important? Psalm 8:4 asks, *"What is man that you are mindful of him, the son of man that you care for him?"* The answer came that God crowned people with glory and honor, put them in charge, visited them and then even died for them in the person of His Son. Just a few minutes of most newscasts tend to dispel any thought of mankind having glory and honor. There are honorable people performing glorious deeds but too many people are cruel to each other, greedily self-centered, in bondage to self-destructive habits, etc.

There is hope. The greatest pursuit a person could have is to get to know this God and develop a relationship with Him. He loves you. He wants what is best for you. He knows how to bring it about.

Let's find the sunny side.

TARDIGRADES

What in the world is a tardigrade? It is a very tiny and very tough aquatic creature. Most of them are less than one mm long (1/25 inch) and have been called water bears or moss piglets.

They have been shown to live through being frozen down to -267^0 C (-452^0F), as well as surviving 151^0C (304^0F). Deep sea divers have to contend with increasing pressure at increasing depths. Fatalities have occurred, yet the tardigrade has been subjected to extreme (600MPa) water pressure six times greater than at the bottom of the deepest ocean trench, without losing its life. X-rays 250 times more intense than those that would kill us simply cause it to curl up, shut down its metabolism, stop its respiration and then bounce back. A special protein labelled Dsup, for damage suppression, provides the protection.

So what?? This was designed, not a chance or random production. The theory of evolution calls for the natural selection of traits that would support survival but cannot account for survival tactics way beyond what it has never, or would ever, encounter. We, and everything around us, are evidences of the amazing provision of a loving Creator.

More information available on Wikipedia.

SAGUARO CACTUS

Is the saguaro cactus a suitable topic for Valentine's Day? It has decorated the landscape of cowboy and western movies for decades, but could it be a fit for this weekend? It is armed with extremely sharp spines, almost as strong as steel needles, which grow to about 7 cm long and have been known to kill a bighorn sheep foolish enough to charge into it. Hardly seems like an emblem of caring.

The saguaro cactus grows almost exclusively in the Sonora Desert areas of Arizona and Mexico. And it grows extremely slowly. After 10 years the sprouted seedling may reach 2 cm, depending on water supply. It can take up to 70 years to reach 2 m (6 ft) and have flowers appear. The tap root will grow 5 feet deep in pursuit of groundwater. A maze of roots will stay within 3" of the surface to trap rain water. Most of the 2000 seeds per flower that aren't eaten by birds still don't survive. Some cacti never produce arms, but most develop them before reaching 100 years. A saguaro can live up to 200 years. Wow!

The main column and the arms develop ribs and pleats that allow the plant to expand with water intake. An adult saguaro may hold a ton of water. Some birds will carve a large hole into the plant, allow the cavity to dry and form a hard shell before using it as a safe nest. Secure apartment condos and hotels?? For centuries people in the area have made jams and jellies from the red fruit and used the strong ribs of dead cacti in construction projects. Inviting shelter and delicious food!

Animals such as bats, bees, insects, lizards, hummingbirds, flickers and finches will come for the flower nectar or fruit. The 3" to 5" flowers bloom for about 24 hours, with about 4 of them opening up every day for a month. Very generous!

It was Andrew Carnegie's philanthropic support in building the Desert Botanical Garden in Tuscon that caused the scientific community to name the saguaro *carnegiea gargantic* in his honor.

Perhaps the saguaro isn't nearly as vicious or inhospitable as it seems. It protects small animals and provides food, water and shelter for many who otherwise might be destitute in the desert. Maybe it is a picture of true love?

Have a lovely time this weekend.

THEME 5

Easter

Is the resurrection really that important?

"And if Christ has not been raised, your faith is futile;
you are still in your sins." 1 Corinthians 15:17

WHAT'S SO GOOD ABOUT GOOD FRIDAY?

A thief appeared before a judge for sentencing because of a robbery. The defendant recognized the judge as a high school buddy and the judge recognized the thief. There was just the hint of a smirk on the thief's face. He was sure of a lenient sentence but the judge handed down the maximum penalty. Then, taking off his robes he walked down to where the defendant stood and said, "I'll pay the debt."

We are approaching Good Friday, the day that reminds us of the crucifixion of Jesus. The Bible claims that He died for you and me. Why would He have to do that? He is offering to pay our debt. What debt is that? Have we done anything deserving capital punishment? We are told in Scripture that death is the earned wage of sin. Somebody has to pay. God is both loving and just, so He exacts the full consequence and then arranges to pay the debt Himself in the person of His Son. That is the most definitive expression of grace. It's getting something really good when we deserved something really bad. That's why it is called Good Friday.

What a gift!

NELLIE'S PALM BRANCH

Just before the Easter season one Sunday is known as Palm Sunday, in memory of the day many Israelites waved palm branches to celebrate the arrival of Jesus in Jerusalem. He was riding on a donkey and the crowds were cheering. It could be that some of the same people were jeering a week later when Jesus was arraigned before Pilate and condemned to die on the cross. They had expected Him to reign as a king instead of die like a criminal. It takes something special to remain true to your leader.

Henry G. Bosch, one of the 60's and 70's editors of the devotional booklet, *Our Daily Bread,* was sorting through his deceased mother's personal effects when he came across a folded piece of paper, yellow with age. Written in his mother's 9 year old childish hand was this note: *"Our Nellie is with the angels now; she is waving a little palm branch in heaven."* Henry Bosch had been told that his mother's 4 year old sister had been an unusually spiritually-oriented child. She often talked about heaven, about saints singing and waving palm branches and especially about Jesus. One day when her father was out of town on a preaching commitment, Nellie became desperately ill with scarlet fever. This attack became so severe that the doctor could do nothing to help. She soon was at the point of death. With insight far beyond her years she told those gathered around her that she would soon be waving *"a little palm branch in heaven."*

This note moved Henry Bosch to tears. Sometimes a child's devotion is unhindered by the cares and troubles of this life.

WAS THE RESURRECTION A HOAX?

Many have claimed that it couldn't happen. It is just a myth. The Romans spread the tale that the body had been stolen by the disciples who then claimed He had come back to life.

Consider the following.

Jesus repeatedly declared that He would be arrested, killed and then rise again after three days. Who can make such a prediction and keep it?

Jesus was publicly executed so that there was no question about whether He actually had died.

The tomb was blocked by a stone that would require several strong men to move it. In addition it was sealed by Roman officials and guarded by soldiers whose lives would be forfeited if the body were to go missing. On the third day they discovered that the tomb was empty and the soldiers were gone.

Jesus was seen alive by many of his disciples and at one point by over 500 at the same time who were available as eyewitnesses.

Previously terrified disciples, who were hiding in fear, were transformed by the resurrection into bold preachers of the gospel. Most of them ended up being persecuted and then executed for their faith. No one would gladly die for something he/she knew wasn't true.

"And if Christ has not been raised, our preaching is useless and so is your faith." 1 Corinthians 15:11

The resurrection of Christ was the evidence God provided that sin's penalty was paid, death had been conquered and Jesus is alive to serve as our Guide and Advocate.

RESURRECTION

Why did there have to be a resurrection? Many people have died horrible, torturous deaths, perhaps as vicious as Jesus endured, but they weren't resurrected. How big is the sacrifice and how necessary is His death if He comes back after three days? There are some good reasons.

A. Death had to be defeated.

The wages of sin is death and Somebody was willing to absorb this consequence. (Romans 6:23) The physical suffering and death was not the main issue. On the cross Jesus took upon Himself the sins of the world. He was saying, "I'll take the rap." Rejecting that leaves a person to pay for it himself/herself. *"The last enemy to be destroyed is death."* 1 Corinthians 15:26

Victory over sin was on the line.

B. Old Testament promises had to be kept.

Is. 53:11 *"After the suffering of His soul He will see the light of life."*

Even though the prediction was an unheard of and humanly impossible feat, God declared it would happen. And it did!

The reliability of Old Testament Scriptures was on the line.

C. Jesus' own predictions had to come true.

Mt. 16:21 *"From that time on Jesus began to explain to his disciples that he must go to Jerusalem and suffer many things at the hands of the elders, the chief priests and the teachers of the law, and that he must be killed and on the third day be raised to life."*

If Jesus was making promises He could not keep, why would we trust Him with our soul?

Jesus' integrity was on the line.

D. His still had intercessory work to do.

1 John 2:2 *"But if anybody does sin, we have an advocate with the Father-Jesus Christ, the Righteous One."* Did you know that Jesus is continually available to intercede for us and every believer on this planet? How could He do this if He was still dead?

Our spiritual well-being was on the line.

E. Our eternal future is at stake.

1 Corinthians 15:17 *"And if Christ has not been raised, your faith is futile, you are still in your sins."* If Jesus had failed in His mission there would be no hope for us either.

Our hope was on the line.

A group of women came to Jesus' tomb just at sunrise on the first day of the week. They found that He was not there. He had risen. It's glorious in the Sonshine!

SIDEWALKS AND EASTER

What does a sidewalk have to do with Easter? There is a connection. One man observed a neighbor using a pressure washer to clean the sidewalk around his house. His own sidewalk was only two feet away. He did not realize how dirty his own sidewalk was until he saw his neighbor's clean one. Now he was keenly aware of the contrast. This motivated him to action. Within days he bought a pressure washer and went to work. What a difference!

Isn't it often that way with ourselves. We don't think that what we are doing is that bad. It's only a small transgression. Who cares? No big deal. We can always think of someone who is worse than we are. It isn't until we come across someone with consistent integrity and love that we realize how unkind our actions really were. It is a big deal! More importantly, how will we fare when we stand in the presence a holy God? The good news is that He has prepared a really great deal for us. He has offered to pay for our sin and give us His righteousness in exchange if we are willing to admit that we need it and humble ourselves enough to ask for it. It's a huge gift!! It's free! That offer is available because of Christ dying on the cross. *"All we like sheep have gone astray. We have turned everyone to his own way and the Lord has laid on Him the iniquity of us all." Isaiah 53:6*

TAKING THINGS FOR GRANTED

I was walking along the Hike & Bike Trail in Oliver, B.C., enjoying the sunshine, birds singing, trees budding, flowers blooming and warmth coming our way. But I took it for granted.

I had a great meal of fruit, vegetables, meat, dessert and beverage. My body was built to get what it needed in nutrients from that meal. My taste buds enjoyed it. I possessed an efficient system for getting rid of what was not beneficial for me. But I took it for granted.

I took a deep breath of fresh air. My lungs were equipped to handle it. The air was just the right mixture of nitrogen and oxygen and other gases. The blood vessels in my lungs and the membranes around the air sacs were just right for allowing oxygen to be absorbed but not the other gases. My red corpuscles were built to transport the oxygen to all my cells where just the right conditions existed to absorb what I needed to fuel the job the cells do. Then the same blood cells were equipped to truck the waste carbon dioxide back to the lungs to be expelled. Without this complex system I would not stay alive. But I took it for granted.

Then I walked past a person having difficulty with something not working right on his bike and he cursed God for it. It struck me how horribly wrong that is and how terrible it is for me to be unthankful. Every day we are provided with a long list of incredibly complex bodily functions and numerous beneficial amenities in the world around us without so much as a thank you coming from us to the Creator. But when some little thing doesn't go just the way we want it we lash out at God. How come He puts up with us? More than that, not only does He put up with us but Easter reminded us that He loved us so much that He sent us His Son to die for us.

We had better take note.

Henry G Wiebe

WHAT HE DID NOT SAY

After the resurrection, when Jesus came to His disciples who were behind locked doors, there are things He could have berated them for. But He didn't! Here are some examples of what He could have said.

What are you doing here, you cowards!

I told you this would happen. Why didn't you believe Me.

After investing over 3 years of my life in you is this the result?

Where were you when I needed you?

You all promised to stick with Me no matter what. But you didn't!

I saw some of the women at the cross, but most of you were not there.

Peter, you've been the leader and you denied you even knew Me. You were scared of the servant girl. How could you?

Have you learned nothing?

If He were to appear in your presence (or mine) right now, would He be able to say some similar things? What He did say to them, and would say to us, is *"Peace be with you."* Be encouraged.

WHO KILLED JESUS?

In my teens I learned a song (*Mickey Holiday, 1970, Singspiration, Inc.*) where part of the chorus contained the following question.

"Who killed Jesus many years ago?
Who was guilty of a crime so low?"

Some might say it was the Roman soldiers. They were a hardened, callous bunch for the most part. They also despised the Jews. Flogging a person destined for crucifixion sometimes brought on death before crucifixion. They drove in the nails and hoisted the cross. Are they guilty? They would respond, "We were only following orders."

Perhaps Pilate should be blamed. He could have set Jesus free. His investigation revealed no reason for such a sentence. His wife also implored him to have nothing to do with this man's death due to a dream she had. But the crowd was incited to demand death for Jesus or he would lose Caesar's support. Pilate relented but also tried to wash his hands of the matter. Hardly innocent but was he the only one?

It must be the Jews who killed him. An illegal, mock trial was held during the night and within hours on the same day Jesus was nailed to the cross. This was against their own Jewish laws. Led by the jealous and hate-filled religious leaders the crowd had been hyped up to demand crucifixion. It worked, so they must be guilty.

The last verse included these words.

> *When I think of Jesus and the way he died,*
> *How upon him all my sins were laid.*
> *All the other people fade away from view.*
> *It's for me the sacrifice was made.*

Jesus' own answer to the question of taking his life is recorded in the Gospel of John.

John 10:18 *"No one takes it from me, but I lay it down of my own accord. I have authority to lay it down and authority to take it up again."*

It was love, not the nails, the soldiers, Pilate or the Jews that kept him on the cross.

THEME 6

Evolution

Is there any possibility that the
hypothesis of evolution is true?

"To suppose that the eye with all its inimitable contrivances for adjusting the focus to different distances, for admitting different amounts of light, and for correction of spherical and chromatic aberration, could have been formed by natural selection, seems, I freely confess, absurd in the highest degree."

*Charles Darwin, Origin of Species (1909
Harvard Classic Edition) p. 190*

BIOMIMETICS - WHAT'S THAT?

When engineers try to copy the design of some features in living creatures they are working in the field of biomimetics. One of the more recent endeavors involves the scaly skin of a sandfish skink lizard. Those scales do not overlap, they allow smooth movement forwards but resist any backward motion and they do all that without any lubrication. What a huge advance this feature would be in miniature devices or those in dusty environments where any oily lubrication would clog things up.

Christian Greuner and Michael Schaefer of the Karlsruhe Institute of Technology in Germany pursued that goal. They copied the scale pattern onto a flat steel surface and tested it out. To their surprise the reduction in friction amounted to 40% less friction! They were hoping for at least 1%. Although the project had consumed many dollars and many hours, their skill in applying it to practical ventures made it very rewarding.

If it took highly developed engineering skill, much money and a lot of time to just copy the idea onto steel, how much more creative skill would the One have who originally incorporated it in a living creature? How is it so many attribute the original design feature to chance and random natural selection, but honor the genius of the ones who copied it? We have a very powerful and highly intelligent Creator. The sandfish lizard's scales were not the product of evolution.

EXACTLY RIGHT

Our solar system within the universe is exactly suitable for life on earth. If any one of the many factors involved were to change in a significant degree or position, we would be annihilated. Just eight examples will be addressed here.

Perfect sunlight

If the sun oscillated in size like many stars do, conditions would be unlivable on earth. The peak intensity of its light is in the infrared spectrum, which provides the warmth we need. Changes in the sun's size would mean too little or too much warmth.

The earth spins at the correct speed

Rotation causes day and night. Longer days and it gets too warm. Longer nights and it gets too cold. Faster rotation would also produce more violent weather conditions than we get now.

The right tilt

The 23.5 degree tilt of the earth's axis creates the seasons for both northern and southern hemispheres. These are vital for food production.

Perfect distance from the sun

If we were 10% closer to the sun, the earth would have furnace-like temperatures. 10% farther away would produce icy deserts. Oceans would either boil off or freeze solid.

Correct orbit of the earth

Earth's orbit is only slightly elliptical. Any less like a circle, like some other planet orbits are, would be devastating to life on earth because of changes in the distance from the sun.

The right size.

Significantly smaller size for earth would reduce gravitational force and the water would be lost into space.

The water cycle

Water covers 70% of the earth's surface, just right for allowing the evaporation, condensation, precipitation and drainage cycle to continually provide water for plants and animals.

Right construction

Earth offers a vast supply of resources such as wood, minerals, animals, plants and a host of other resources that are useful for mankind. In addition, earth has the right conditions to permit the formation and maintenance of the ozone layer in the atmosphere to protect us. It has a magnetic field which helps to deflect harmful radiation from the sun, and aids navigation. Our atmosphere is composed of just the right gases, unlike some of the noxious combinations found elsewhere in our solar system.

We need to be immensely grateful to our Creator for getting it just right for us. So why isn't everything perfect on earth? We misuse and abuse what we've been given in Creation and in moral principles.

FIGS, FIG WASPS AND FIGMENTS

The symbiotic relationship between the fig wasp and <u>certain varieties</u> of figs is amazing. A symbiotic relationship is one in which both participants benefit from, or are even dependent on, each other for survival.

Figs are actually like an inverted flower. All the reproductive parts (stamen, pistil, pollen) are inside the growing fig. A female fig wasp that hatches inside this certain fig emerges carrying pollen and seeks a different fig of the same kind, likely on a different tree, where she can lay her eggs. This fig (syconium) has a narrow opening at the tip (ostiole) through which she enters the fig, usually losing her wings and antenna as she squeezes through. Doesn't matter. She won't need them anymore because she will die after laying eggs. If she is fortunate enough to have chosen a male fig (caprifig) she'll find just the right setup for laying her eggs, which will hatch into larvae and grow into male and female wasps. Males are blind and wingless. They will mate with the females, bore holes in the fig's skin for the females to escape and serve no other purpose. (Guys, they are not our male role models!!) They'll die inside the fig, be digested by fig enzymes and never leave the fig or see the light of day. Most commercial varieties of figs for human consumption are self-pollinating, no digested wasps in them.

If the female wasp happens to enter a female fig it will pollinate the fig to produce seeds but its own eggs and the female wasp will starve to death and be digested by the fig. It has no escape available.

Isn't it amazing that such a complex relationship exists? Some people believe that it took millions of years for this relationship to develop by evolution. Think of all the pieces that would have to fall into place, by accident at the same time, for this to be true. It has to all be there at once.

1. It would require accidently developing male and female figs to be in place, complete with pollen, stamens, pistils, ostiole openings, genetic instructions in the DNA and a myriad of support mechanisms, to produce the seeds to grow the tree before it can produce any figs. How do you do that?
2. At the same time we would need accidently developed male and female wasps complete with all the abilities to produce eggs, to mate, to be programmed to find the other fig if the wasp is a female, programmed to bore holes if a male, be genetically equipped to grow from egg to larvae to adult and to reproduce. A tough sell!
3. Time is not the friend of evolution. It is the enemy. Everything has to come together in exactly the right

condition and in the same place and at the same time fully formed. You can't have some parts wait millions of years for the other parts to show up.

4. One evolutionist stated that both the fig wasp and the fig have the same goal, so it all comes together. Neither one has the ability to plan progress toward a goal. The theory of atheistic evolution does not allow for any goals, purpose or design features. It is all by random mutations and chance. Natural selection requires the presence of something to select from and the intelligence to select what fits, which it doesn't have. Would I be resorting to a FIGment of the imagination to accept that?

5. Last, this same challenge of having every 'piece' in place exists for every one of the millions of plant and animal species. The cumulative probability factor is astronomically exponential, infinitely great. Totally impossible.

The process and design was the work of the Creator, and it is amazing.

SIR FREDERIC HOYLE

Sir Frederic Hoyle, British astronomer and mathematician, when challenged by fellow scientists who were claiming that living particles could come together and create life, made the following response.

Anyone with even a nodding acquaintance with the Rubik cube will concede the near impossibility of a solution being obtained by a blind person moving the cube faces at random. Now imagine 10 to the power of 50 (that is 10 followed by fifty zeroes) blind persons standing shoulder to shoulder, (these would more than fill our entire planetary system) each with a scrambled Rubik cube and try to conceive of the chance of them all simultaneously arriving at the solved form.

You then have the chance of arriving by random shuffling (random variation) of just one of the many bio-polymers on which life depends. The notion that not only the bio-polymers but the operating program of a living cell could be arrived at by chance in a primordial soup here on Earth is evidently nonsense of a high order. Life must plainly be a cosmic phenomenon.

Hoyle was an agnostic, which basically means doubting, or not made my mind up. He tried to make up an argument that life came from outer space but gave up on the idea realizing that the same problem arises in a primordial pond on another planet, and would still be a 10 to the 50th power of chance.

Hoyle's quotes were taken from the book,
In the Minds of Men by Ian Taylor.

*Sir F. Hoyle, 1981, from The Big Bang in
Astronomy, New Scientist magazine.*

HUMMINGBIRDS

Hummingbirds are amazing. Their size, beauty and even aggressiveness are only outdone by their agility. They can fly forwards, backwards, up, down and even hover while beating their wings 50 – 80 times a second. Huge breast muscles make up 40% of the bird's weight. Ounce for ounce some of them must be among the most aggressive fighters when it comes to food.

Wing design is very specialized. Where other birds have something like elbow and wrist joints, hummingbirds have a rigid structure, making it more like a stiff paddle. Not only are the bones, muscles and tendons that operate the wings uniquely designed, but the brain and nervous system that control these are very specialized.

Biochemical engineers have attempted to duplicate this complex system of biomechanical wonders but in spite spending huge amounts of time and money they have not been successful. If they did achieve this, it would simply prove that hummingbirds did not happen by chance and natural selection but by very intelligent design.

Hummingbirds are a marvelous design by a Creator.

AMAZING BIRD MIGRATIONS

Along the Atlantic Coast, from the Maritime Provinces to Cape Cod in Massachusetts, the autumn flights of millions of land birds signal their migration south. The puzzling thing is that these land birds are heading out to sea! Birds of different kinds and sizes are heading for the Caribbean (2900 km) or even South America (3700 km). The only possible landing spot in between is Bermuda, about 1300 km or about twenty hours flying time. MOST DON'T EVEN STOP THERE! They pass over it at about two km up in the air. Many don't even stop on a Caribbean island but carry on to South America for a non-stop flight of 80-90 hours!!

How can they do that? Some don't survive and become food for ocean creatures. Plovers and sandpipers are known to fly non-stop. Some birds weighing less than an ounce do it. Why would they choose the sea route when they could follow the land and find rest along the way like some other birds do? The sea route is much shorter. How did they know that? Flying at altitudes of four to six km high avoids predators and catches favorable wind currents. Who told them that?

What about fuel for the trip? The tiny Blackpoll Warbler, weighing less than two loonies, uses about 1/3 ounce of fat for the trip. That would be about 400,000 km per liter. Fantastic gas mileage. Biologist Ryan Norris, University of Guelph, clocked five warblers averaging 62 km/hr over a flight of 2540 km. The Golden Plover migrates from Nova Scotia to South America with weight loss from six ounces down to four ounces for the 3700 km flight. That's one ounce of fuel for about 900 km! With upper atmosphere winds behind them some were clocked at 167-185 km/hr using tiny, attached electronic devices. Hummingbirds have been judged to use 1/10 ounce of fuel for the 800 km crossing of the Gulf of Mexico. The Arctic Tern has the longest migration of all, 42,000 km return trip annually from the Arctic to the Antarctic.

These abilities and programmed routes did not develop by chance, mutations and natural selection as evolution claims. We labor long and hard to not do things by chance. Mutations are mistakes in the DNA. Selection demands that there is a purposeful process of choosing. None of these make sense as an evolutionary process. These abilities were created by a very powerful and very intelligent Designer. Our Creator is amazing.

MITCHELL'S JOURNEY
(PART 1 OF 7)

Mitchell lay on the ground tearing away at the grass in frustration. Neither the sky above nor the scenery around him were of interest. Parading through his mind was a replay of that afternoon's interaction between him and his friend. It had started so innocently. Mitchell had invited his friend Sam to come with him to hear a prominent evolutionist speaker on their university campus. He thought it would demolish the ideas of creationists like Sam. He was looking for a knock-out blow in that lecture.

Sam had answered, "Really? What was that knock-out blow?"

"We don't need a god to explain the existence of the universe," replied Mitchell.

"Tell me," responded Sam, "why is there something instead of nothing?"

"What has that got to do with it?" queried Mitchell.

"A lot," responded Sam. "How did we and everything else around us get here?"

"A singularity exploded and the rest is history," Mitchell had replied.

"Really? And what was that singularity? How did it get here along with all the laws of nature and science needed for an explosion to occur?" Sam had remained very calm but Mitchell was getting irked. "Well I guess it was just there."

"Mitch, I sense that you are getting upset," responded Sam. "I want you to know that I am not against you. I'm interested in finding out what is based on sound logic, matches reality, does not conflict with established laws of science and nature and gives meaning to life. Then I'll have the truth."

"OK, OK. I get it," conceded Mitch.

"So, a self-existent piece of something had the capability of producing the entire huge, complex and intricate universe, including us, by exploding. But an all-powerful, superbly intelligent, self-existent Being is not acceptable as the creator of it all?"

Mitchell struggled to respond. "So where did this God come from?"

"I guess we have to choose between a self-existent, inanimate singularity exploding or a self-existent, super-intelligent God creating," answered Sam. "It's a question of what was the **first cause**. May I explain how I feel about that?"

"Alright," responded Mitchell somewhat grudgingly. "Go ahead and try." Sam proceeded with his answer.

"Both the theories of creation and evolution are faced with the question of how it got started. We can envision an eternally self-existing God capable of designing everything that exists or postulate a god of some kind who kick-started the process and left it for evolution to carry on. Or we could imagine that it all started by itself from noth- ꞏ ingness that condensed into a very small singularity and exploded with a big bang to form everything. In that option we are faced with the idea that if you start with nothing and wait long enough, then by chance and natural selection you will get everything. That I find to be truly untenable. Starting with self-existing inanimate matter instead of nothingness capable of turning itself into living things and all else that we have is also unexplainable. Is that self-existent "matter" a god? If God pre-programmed the development it is no longer by chance and therefore not evolution. The only logical choice is an eternally self-existent person, God, capable of creation. In life we consistently look for cause and design. Why should we then conclude that the universe is without cause or design?"

Mitchell had left without knowing what else to say and it angered him. Now, here on the grass he was faced with his parting words to Sam. "I'll straighten you out on that one next time we meet." Then he had an idea.

MITCHELL'S JOURNEY
PART 2 OF 7

Mitchell was almost eager to share his idea when he met Sam again. His answer was that he would stick with the idea of an eternally self-existent piece of matter from which everything around us had generated and Sam could rely on his idea of an eternally self-existent Creator. That would put them on equal footing for what Mitchell still thought of as a battle.

"Fair enough," replied Sam. "We'll take it from there."

Sometime later their geology class went on an archeological field trip. On a shale slope one person discovered an arrowhead. The professor pointed out that its shape, cutting edge and notch for a shaft were conclusive evidence that it had been designed by a hunter or warrior for a purpose. We can learn a lot about an ancient culture from one artifact.

Sam spoke up and asked, "How is it that 3 facts about a piece of rock form conclusive evidence of a designer but a vastly more intricate and complex universe isn't acceptable evidence for a **Designer**?"

"You can believe in a Creator-God if you want but science has ruled that out," was the reply.

"I believe science does the opposite of that. May I explain why I say that?" requested Sam. With permission granted Sam continued, "Science relies on the predictability of reactions in such things as chemistry, physics and the structure of nature's laws. That requires programmed design. Our universe from the tiniest cell to the outer galaxies is full of intricate systems and complicated organization that infinitely outweighs the simple facts of shape, size and sharpness used as evidence for the design in an arrowhead. How can we then conclude there was no designer behind our universe? If a few features in an arrowhead show design for a purpose how can we conclude infinitely more complex features in living things came about without a Designer or a purpose?

"Believe what you like," declared the professor. "I don't buy into that conclusion. Evolution has shown that changes over time have produced all there is. It's happening right now. Get with the times, Mitchell."

"What do you start with?" asked Sam.

"The Big Bang explosion," remarked the professor. "Now let's get on with why we are here."

Mitchell sensed victory ahead.

MITCHELL'S JOURNEY
PART 3 OF 7

Back at home Mitchell was no longer frustrated about not being able to give Sam a good answer. That archeologist had put Sam in his place. He now had the answer he needed. With enthusiasm he picked up the phone and called Sam. "Hey Sam, are you game for a walk? I've got the answer to the problem of achieving design. It'll show how evolution can happen."

"Glad to hear what you have to say, Mitch. I'll be there in a bit."

After only a few steps along the way Sam asked, "So what have you got, Mitch? I'm intrigued."

"**Mutations**, Sam. Mutations! That's how it works. There are tiny changes bit by bit over millions of years. The best ones survive and you've got one species changing into a new and better one. See, it's simple!"

"Mitch! Do you know what mutations are? They are mistakes in the code, in the DNA. Those mistakes consist of omissions, reversals, spelling mistakes. You're telling me that we and everything around us are the product of mistakes?"

"I don't care what they are. I'm just convinced that they make changes."

"Mutations makes changes alright, usually negative or even lethal ones. We get deformed births, missing parts and often fatal results.

In order for improvement to happen there would have to be information added to the DNA code. Mutations are deletions from the code or mistakes in the blueprint. You don't get improvement changes that way. No one has ever found that a mutation adds information or redesigns the code to a new and improved version."

"Are you sure about that?"

"Yes! The DNA of a living organism contains the programmed instructions for its development. In humans the first cell at conception in the mother's womb contains a 6 foot strand. That cell is the size of a period at the end of a sentence. It is estimated by some scientists (including non-Christians) that these instructions in that cell would fill about 500 volumes of an encyclopedia. When the cell splits to form two, a copy of the instructions is made. The DNA then acts as a project superintendent to direct various cells to form the organs, nerves, bones, etc., in just the right place in the right order and at the right time. Amazing!! This process produces not millions, not billions, but **trillions** of cells each programmed to fulfill a specific function. I appreciate your earnestness in searching for answers, Mitch, but this one doesn't cut it. Mutations subtract information, evolution requires adding new information and redesigning the organism, therefore mutations cannot accomplish evolution."

"I'm not giving up, Sam. There has yet to be a good reason why so many scientists support evolution. We'll get you cornered eventually."

MITCHELL'S JOURNEY
PART 4 OF 7

At home Sam thought to himself, "There's something more that I should tell Mitch. He is sincere about finding the truth. I'll email him."

*"Mitch, I appreciate the commitment you show to discovering what's right. Therefore I feel free to add something to what I told you in the last few weeks. The whole premise of survival of the fittest on which evolution depends demands that enough is present all at the same time for something like an organ to appear and thrive. It's called **irreducible complexity**. A part in a motor missing, a cable for a computer not there, a section of the optic nerve gone renders each one non-functional. Even a simple thing like a mouse trap has to have all the essential parts present or it is useless. You can't have one part appear by accident and then wait for thousands or millions of years for the next part to appear. That partly formed item would be gone as quick as it came.*

Not only does one organ or feature have to be complete all at once in order to function, there are untold millions of complex systems and organs in the inanimate and animate world that must be in place in there totality or the item will not even form. The idea of hanging on to the beginnings of an eye until after millions of years the optic nerves and receptor brain cells just happen to develop to match it, is preposterous. The level of complexity is such that if anything is missing from the system it will not work. The mathematical probability of any of those millions of organisms or structures coming into place by chance is effectively zero.

In Darwin's day the cell was thought to be a very simple blob of proto-plasm. Not so! Remember what I told you earlier? You started in your mother's womb as a one-celled zygote the size of a period at the end of this sentence. In that cell a six foot coiled-up strand contained all the coded information, the computer software program that determined who and what you would become as a human being. Hardly a simple cell. Think about what that means, Mitch. Crucial components in non-living structures and critical organs in living organisms have to occur in completed form immediately to work. They cannot slowly develop over millions of years one part at a time. I'm not trying to put you down, Mitch. I just want to get at the truth."

Mitchell puzzled and agonized a bit over that one. He decided to check with an expert. He was sure there would be an answer, and he'd find it.

MITCHELL'S JOURNEY
PART 5 OF 7

Mitchell did study and think about what Sam had shared with him over the last few weeks. He decided to question his university professor about the subject in hopes of gaining some insight. He asked for an appointment.

"Sir, in class we've talked about the assumed process of evolution over vast periods of time. The chance mutations and natural selection process would produce small changes over time, resulting in transitional forms by the millions for all living things. Yet I read that few if any conclusively transitional life forms have ever appeared in the fossil record. Do they even exist?"

"There have been some fossil finds that could be transitional forms," replied the professor.

"But," declared Mitchell, "There are those who claim that if evolution were true we should find not just **a** missing link but millions of them. Furthermore, since evolution is a very slow process they say that we should have multitudes of transitional forms living on earth today. Instead we have well-defined species reproducing after their kind with variation within the species. Apparently the pre-Cambrian layer has revealed an explosion of fully formed fossils with no transitional forms found. By their own admission some prominent evolutionists have agreed that this issue is a major hurdle for them."

"We're still looking."

"It disturbed me to read that some so-called transitional humanoid forms have been built up from a tooth or a jawbone or a collection of small bones and proved fraudulent but still used as evidence. There should be many millions of failed transitional forms if evolution were true."

"As I said, we're still looking," replied the professor.

Mitchell left his office disappointed. Now what? Where do I go from here?

It's important to be guided by answers you can't question instead of questions you can't answer.

MITCHELL'S JOURNEY
PART 6 OF 7

Doubts increased for Mitchell during a class study of entropy. Known as the Second Law of Thermodynamics, it plainly says that left to itself everything deteriorates or randomizes. What was organized or well-ordered becomes disordered. Without influence from outside itself the entity degenerates. The professor credited the sun with being the outside energy source to not only prevent that for our planet but even bring about a reversal of the effect.

Mitchell decided to hear Sam's version of how entropy plays into this question. Sam was glad to reply.

"We battle entropy every time we try to maintain something in working order. When our bodies age due to genetic entropy we try to prolong the inevitable. Nothing can produce new and improved versions all by itself. We have frequently heard comments in the media of how "mother nature developed this" or how a particular animal took "millions of years to develop" whatever. Who is "mother nature" and what animal can redesign itself? The Second Law of Thermodynamics is the opposite of what evolution requires. It is evolution not creation that is in conflict with science here.

There are those who rightfully point out that it is only in a closed system that this happens. An open system can receive energy from outside itself and thereby increase in complexity as that outside source loses energy. They would say the sun provides that for our planet, thereby over-riding entropy. However, the sun is only part of the picture. For plants to grow and reproduce the whole process of photosynthesis, osmosis, reproduction and nutrient absorption from the soil has to already exist. The water cycle, the carbon dioxide cycle and a myriad of other life-sustaining processes have to exist before the sun can be of any help. Without them the sun is more likely to kill life and produce a Sahara Desert.

Not only that, how did the sun happen to be just the right distance from earth for life to be supported, and the earth's axis tilted just right to allow for seasons and the atmosphere composed of just the right combination of gases and the nature of water be just right for the water cycle to function? These and many other demands make the sun a completely untenable option for negating entropy all by itself. The only outside energy force that could bring about such changes is the Creator."

A troubled Mitchell went home to think about what had just been said.

MITCHELL'S JOURNEY
CONCLUSION

Shortly after that last conversation with Sam, Mitchell was jolted by the professor's reminder to the class. In a few weeks their second planned invitational guest lecture would be taking place. Mitchell had spearheaded campus advertising and MC'd the first event. It was paramount that the committee meet this week to finalize plans for the promotion of atheistic evolution on campus.

"So, Mitchell," asked the professor, "when can we meet?"

Mitchell was stunned by the request, even though he had earlier agreed to it. "I –I don't think I'm the right person for the job," he stammered.

"I was wondering about you, Mitchell, ever since your questions about transitional forms! Who's been brainwashing you?" exclaimed the professor. "You've been the main student force behind these events. What happened?"

"Sir," he replied in a steadier, bolder tone. "I've been thinking, reading, studying and discussing the validity of the theory of evolution and, yes, I have developed some serious doubts about it." The class responded in a chorus of shocked unbelief.

"How could you! What doubts?" demanded the professor. "Be specific."

"OK," replied Mitchell, "I'll list my concerns."

The materialistic naturalism of the atheistic evolutionist gives no explanation for how everything got here and why we are here. It assumes the existence of matter and all the laws of nature and science. The emergence of life is seen as an unexplained cosmic accident or self-organizing event. None of this makes sense. All of the above relies on the supernatural, very supernatural, yet the evolutionary worldview denies the supernatural.

Evolution from simple life forms to very complex ones is said to happen without purpose, plan or design. Yet, in real life we constantly rely on purpose, plan or design for most of what we do. Evolution does not match reality.

Evolution claims that random mutations (which are mistakes, omissions or misspellings in the genetic code) and natural selection (selection implies an intelligence that chooses) over long periods of time will eventually result in the incredibly complex and fine-tuned, very balanced, universe where all systems are interdependent and supportive of each other. Yet in real life designers have to work long and hard to produce workable equipment or systems. Their goal is to leave nothing to chance. Evolution leaves much to chance. Think of the years of highly skilled work and the billions of dollars spent on the Challenger shuttle. One faulty O-ring caused the whole enterprise to blow up on Jan. 28, 1986. The 7 astronauts in it died due to one mistake. Can we be the product of random events and numerous mistakes?

Evidence of such development is presumed to support evolution from one kind of plant or animal via transitional forms. Scant are the proposed examples that are claimed to show this and many of these were proven fraudulent. If gradual transitions from one species or kind to another had been happening there would be no distinctions allowing us to identify species. The boundaries would all be a blur.

The Second Law of Thermodynamics states that the entropy of a closed system tends to a maximum, which means it degenerates unless an outside energy feeds into it to counteract that. The sun is suggested as that energy source but is only one agent in the whole enterprise. Without such things as the water cycle, photosynthesis, DNA, carbon oxygen cycle, etc. already in place the sun just produces a Sahara Desert, not improved living things.

Without purpose, plan or design there can be no such thing as right or wrong, good or bad, evil or kind. Yet we have libraries full of laws, courtrooms for judges and lawyers, fleets of security officials and huge police forces in an attempt to see justice done. But evolution is amoral. This does not mean that evolutionists are automatically immoral. There are many who believe in evolution that live morally upright lives but creationists say that is not caused by evolution but because they have been created with a conscience.

Some creationists claim that the difference between the two theories can be expressed in two ways.

Atheistic Evolution

If we start with nothing and wait long enough then by mutations and natural selection we will get everything there is.

Creation

A Creator in the beginning designed what exists with the potential for variation within kinds (multiple species form a kind).

Mitchell concluded, "I'm beginning to wonder if I'm the one who's deceived."

(I leave it to your imagination as to what followed in that class. But for each one of us individually this is not an imaginary challenge but a real life issue.)

The sunny side pictures a Creator who loves you and tells you the truth.

THERE PROBABLY IS NO GOD??

Back in 2009, many of us saw the TV news clip that showed London buses with signs claiming that there probably is no God. The lady who instigated the campaign said there was no scientific evidence that God exists. Science depends heavily on observation of the facts. I have observed the following.

Our life depends on access to air. A few minutes without it and we are dead. It just so happens that we are surrounded by it in just the right composition of nitrogen, oxygen and other gases. Our planet has the gravity to keep it from dispersing into space and our bodies have the respiratory system that is just right for using it. That's no accident.

Without water we'd be dead in days. It just so happens that this planet has lots of it, even to the point where the water cycle and natural earth filters continually purify it from the pollutants we give it. Our bodies have the digestive and circulatory systems just right for using it. Not only that, it is a remarkable solvent and cleansing agent. Contrary to most liquids, water expands when it freezes. If that didn't happen ice would sink and successive layers would reduce all lakes and rivers to solid ice killing everything in it. How nice!!

All around us we have fruit, vegetables and meat sources just right for our bodies' needs. We are equipped with a digestive and elimination system that extracts what we need and disposes of the rest. Our circulation system is equipped with a red corpuscle transportation system to deliver the nutrients where needed. How remarkably fortuitous this is!!

Our planet's axis is tilted at just the right angle to give us seasons. The sun is just the right distance away and the revolutions and rotations of planet earth provide us with night and day plus the seasons we crucially need. Again, how would we survive without this?

Our bodies are equipped with senses for our use and survival. The human brain capacity was there long before computers. Then we use this brain to decide that no one planned or designed all of the above and a multitude of other amazing benefits. Can you believe that??? The evidence is clear!

ONE DROP OF WATER

One drop of water was enough. Enough of what? Enough evidence to bring about a conclusion. Let's backtrack a bit and get a picture of what is at stake.

I was in a university Chemistry class where the professor was dealing with the significance of how the water molecule was formed. I knew that it was made up of two hydrogen atoms and one atom of oxygen but what I didn't know really piqued my interest. Apparently the two hydrogen atoms are attached to the oxygen atom at a 105 degree angle. So what? This configuration brings on a result that is crucial to our existence. Most, if not all, liquids contract when they freeze. Because of the angle in the molecule of water it expands when it freezes. That's why a bottle of water, or a hose with water in it, or even a car's radiator, splits when it freezes. That doesn't sound like good news crucial to our existence but wait. Since water expands when it freezes into ice its density is less than the liquid and it floats. Think of what would happen if it contracted and became heavier than liquid water of the same volume. It would sink. Quite aside from the fact that it would ruin the whole idea of skating on a pond or lake, it would cover the bottom of the lake with successive layers of ice. That would kill animal and plant life in that lake and increasingly trap water in a prison of ice. Eventually the whole ecosystem would be adversely affected, perhaps so severely as to destroy much of the life on this planet.

We can't live without a constant reliable source of water. Furthermore, there is no liquid available on earth that is as efficient and effective a solvent as water. We take for granted that its availability and power to absorb is simply there without giving a thought to why it was designed that way or who designed it just the way we need it. It certainly did not happen by chance as the hypothesis of evolution claims.

Psalm 106:1 *"Praise the LORD. Give thanks to the LORD, for he is good; his love endures forever."*

OWLS

Owls are uniquely equipped to survive. Some of those marvels are listed here.

Vision is keen, even at night. They cannot move their eyes, therefore can only see a 110 degree arc. However, they can rotate their head about three quarters of the way around to compensate for eyes that don't move. That would be a fatal move for us. Furthermore, their eyes have more rod cells than cone cells allowing them to see three times better than us in the dark. This is enhanced by a lining in the eye called *tapetum lucidem* which bounces light back to the rods for an extended look. If you shine a light on their eyes it glows yellow or green because of that layer.

Hearing is so keen that they can detect faint sounds. Some species have one ear lower than the other allowing them to better detect where the sound is coming from. The ears are not where you'd think they would be. The tufts on their head serve a different purpose. The face is a cupped shape to catch sounds. That facial disc of feathers acts like a satellite dish to catch sound waves. Additionally the head can turn nearly all the way around to catch those sounds. Some owls can hear a vole under 18 inches of snow from 60 feet away.

Wings and feathers are designed for silent flight. Wings are shaped like an airfoil to produce lift with fewer movements. Slower, quieter flight is then possible making the capture of rodents easier. Wing feathers are specially designed to reduce noise in that specialized fringes break the air stream into small currents.

Prey most often consists of mice and voles. An owl needs about three to four small rodents a day. In their 10 year life span about 12,000 rodents would have been eaten by them. These rodents would have consumed about fifteen tons of grain from grain farms. Maybe owls are a farmer's best friend.

Although owls don't often form a flock, a group is called a parliament of owls. There is a saying about being wise as an owl, even though their collective wisdom doesn't seem to call for a parliamentary session very often. But we can be very sure of one thing, it was not the 'wisdom' of the owls that developed these features. It was the superbly high intelligent design of our Creator.

A "SIMPLE" CELL?

A century or more ago people thought that the human cell was just a blob of protoplasm. The truth is described in the next paragraphs.

We now know that every single living cell is so complex that it is virtually beyond our ability to describe it. We could for example, compare it to a miniature "city" but the comparison would be inadequate because cities cannot reproduce themselves as cells can. However, the "city" is still a useful analogy. The cell's tiny factories constantly retrieve, process and store food, while highly efficient power plants burn it, producing (and storing) energy without overheating the delicate, temperature-sensitive molecular mechanisms. Meanwhile, an elaborate "communication network" allows instant communication inside and outside the cell. The transport systems and waste disposal systems are models of efficiency. All this machinery is manufactured to high precision from the raw materials of nutrient molecules – and the entire city can reproduce itself in a matter of minutes! How could something so complex arise by chance, random processes?

That question remains one of the great mysteries for those who think that life arose out of the disorder of a "big bang". No one today would presume that modern factories arose by way of an explosion in a brickyard; so if cells are more complex than cities, then their origin begs for even greater intelligent design.

Machines require a blueprint, and blueprints require a designer. In all living things this blueprint is written on DNA... DNA carries the code (or instructions) for every "machine" within the cells, telling them what to make... The DNA molecule is the most compact and efficient storage information system in the known universe. For example, the amount of information that could be stored in a single pinhead of DNA would be equivalent to a pile of paper back novels 240 times as high as the distance from the earth to the moon, or 100,000,000 times more information than a 40 gigabyte hard drive could hold on your computer.

Quoted from Alien Intrusion by Gary Bates, 2004 p. 120-121

WATER STRIDERS

As a child I sometimes watched these spider-like creatures skate across the top of a pond on the farm. I thought little of it besides just assuming they were too light to sink. I knew nothing about the surface tension of water that creates an invisible "skin" as the water molecules at the top "cling" to each other. This same tension causes water droplets to form a bead on surfaces like glass. They don't flatten out like most liquids.

Robotics engineers have sought to copy that insect's ability. Perhaps they could create a small enough surveillance device or drone capable of the water strider's feats. In 2005 robotics engineers reported the production of the first robot to mimic the water strider's ability to skate on water. This field of study is called biomimetics, and the production of these robots is biorobotics. However there is still a long way to go. The strider can jump up to six times as high as its own length, then land safely without crashing or sinking. Man-made robots still either crash on land or sink on water. David Catchpoole declares that the hurdles to overcome include the following ones.

> *Ten years on and researchers, intent on copying the leaping prowess of the water strider, have made impressive progress. Using high speed cameras and other equipment, the researchers observed that the water strider's legs accelerate gradually, so that the surface of the water does not retreat too quickly (which would mean losing contact). They found that the maximum force exerted by the water strider's legs approaches, but never exceeds, the opposing vertical component of the water's surface tension (and therefore the legs don't sink). They also observed that the water striders sweep their legs inward to lengthen the time period they can push against the surface of the water. Furthermore the curved tips of their legs are just the right shape to adapt to the dimples that form on the water's surface when the legs push downwards, thus enhancing to the fullest possible extent the surface tension on the legs. All of this maximizes the overall force for their jumps.*

The water strider didn't decide to develop this nor did it come by accident or chance mutations. It was wonderfully designed by a Very Intelligent Designer.

There are so many wonderful things in nature that honor the Creator.

Based on a Creation magazine article, Vol. 39, No. 3, 2017

THEME 7

Forgiveness

Is receiving and giving complete forgiveness actually possible?

"If we confess our sins, he is faithful and just and will forgive us our sins and purify us from all unrighteousness." 1 John 1:9

CAN TWO JAILED ENEMIES FIND PEACE?

We hear a fair bit about hope for peace on earth especially when we approach the Christmas season. Thus far neither the season nor the hopes have produced it. We wish they had. But there is an astoundingly true story of two mortal enemies who found peace and became very dear friends.

Evelyn Christenson tells a remarkable story about leading a prayer seminar in war-torn Belfast in June of 1981. The conflict between Protestant and Catholic antagonists was severe. Liam and Jimmy were both in prison for their acts of terrorism but they were on opposite sides of the conflict. In an interview with her, Liam spoke of his "dirty protests" and rebellious actions in prison, including a 56 day hunger strike that brought him to the brink of death. His praying mother succeeded in getting the prison officials to use intravenous feeding to spare his life. Ten other prisoners in the hunger strike had already died. After recovering, Liam was put into solitary confinement for a while with a Bible as the only reading material. It changed his view on life. He decided to trust in Jesus as Savior and Lord.

Jimmy watched the transformation with amazement. He now wanted what Liam had. He ended up making the same decision. They began studying the Bible and praying together. As Liam put it, "I used to be willing to shoot him dead but now I would die for him." Few people have that dramatic a story but the truth of the following verse is available to all. Then there is a solution to conflict.

2 Corinthians 5:17 *"Therefore, if anyone is in Christ, the new creation has come: The old has gone, the new is here!"*

That is an astounding and effective way to find peace!

Evelyn Christenson, What Happens When God Answers, p.4

BOUGHT BACK

"My bike is gone," exclaimed a tearful Timmy. "I can't find it anywhere. Somebody's taken it!" A search by father and son failed to locate the bike anywhere in the neighborhood. Later, visits to several pawnshops did locate the missing bike, but since the family had failed to put any undeniable identifying marks on it, they couldn't claim it or involve the police. The father had to buy it from the shop. The bike had to be redeemed, purchased a second time.

It's a whole lot like our relationship to God. He has provided us with a vast array of benefits, provisions and things to enjoy, far beyond the value of a bike. Through the inroads of sin we lost any claim to these benefits or the relationship to God that we were designed to have. But they are offered to us anyway. Should we then just take everything we have for granted and even complain when we don't get more or better? Hardly a thought of thanksgiving crosses the minds of many people. As we approach Good Friday we are reminded of what it cost the Lord to buy us back, to pay the price for our redemption. His promise still is that *"Everyone who calls on the name of the Lord will be saved." Romans 10:13*

A CALL FROM THE DARKNESS

One more night. One more life in peril. The mother had swallowed an overdose of pills. Could she be reached in time to save her life?

"Hello? Can I help you?" Silence on the other end of the telephone line.

"Are you there?" I said again. "I'm here to help you."

Finally, a woman's voice responded, "Yes...I'm here."

"It sounds like you're really struggling with something," I continued. "I can help."

"I don't think anyone can help me now." She hesitated. Each passing second seemed like an eternity. The voice, faint yet audible, continued. "They're sound asleep now. They'll be much better off without me. I just can't take the darkness."

Through her sobs, I could feel the stinging pain the woman carried for past mistakes and broken relationships. She had bathed her two children, ages three and six, put them into their pyjamas and then tucked them in. Unlike other nights, she found herself kneeling beside their beds, praying for their protection and safety, and for forgiveness. Moments later, she left their room, swallowed a hundred pills and called The Salvation Army's suicide crisis line. She was scared and didn't want to die alone. It was 3:43 a.m.

"Hang in there with me." Her breathing was laboured, her voice faint. "Can you tell me where you are? I want to send an ambulance to help you." She paused, hesitant to tell me anything.

"It's going to be over soon," she uttered. "I just can't take the darkness anymore."

"Oh, Lord," I prayed. "It's the middle of the night. I'm alone on the phone speaking with a woman who is dying. I'm not worthy of this task. Why have you asked me to meet her at this crossroad? Lord, help her."

Time was of the essence. The woman seemed to know it and so did I. From what she told me, I knew that the pills she ingested would rob her of her life in a very short time.

"Can you hear me? Come on, stay with me!" Silence.

Then, faintly, I heard her whisper, "I'm here."

"You're not alone." I pressed. "I know you're hurting, but your children need you, they need their Mom. I'm going to help you, OK?"

In her pain, she'd convinced herself that the children would only think she was asleep. She thought the six-year-old would know enough to go to the neighbours across the hall for help.

"Is your front door open?" I asked. "How will your children get to the neighbours?" Her breathing was becoming increasingly laboured.

"Listen to me. Your children need you."

Suddenly, she cried, "Oh, no, what have I done?"

Yes! A breakthrough! She'd seen the light amidst inescapable darkness.

"You can do this"

With cellphone in one hand and cordless phone in the other, I called 9-1-1. Although her life was slipping away, she rallied enough to give me the details I needed to direct the emergency response unit to her apartment. "They'll be there any second," I assured her. Suddenly, I heard the woman fall down a flight of stairs. Silence. Then…I could hear her breathing! "You can do this. You're doing a great job!" I encouraged. "Stephanie, I fell."

"I can hear you. You're going to be OK. I'm still here!" Sirens wailed in the distance. I heard footsteps running, voices yelling. "Hello, this is the police—we've got her. We'll take it from here."

When the paramedics found her, the woman was unconscious but still alive. Her body lay at the front door of the two-storey walk-up. The ambulance crew was amazed she had been able to reach up, unlatch the door and find enough strength to prop it open so they could get in. They said they never would have gotten to her in time if she hadn't worked so hard to stay alive.

It was 3:56 a.m. Hanging up the phone, I felt such relief. I thanked God for giving this stranger the will to keep living and for entrusting me with such an awesome responsibility. The silence of that night wasn't so deafening anymore. The cries of a desperate young mother had broken through the darkness. God had heard her and responded.

*Written by Stephanie Oliver, a worker at the
Salvation Army's suicide crisis centre.*

CLEAN SLATE

Most of us will have heard the expression: *wipe the slate clean.* The following illustration demonstrates how that expression originated.

Many years ago school children were provided with a thin stone slab as a writing surface. It was called a slate and you wrote on it with a slate pencil. Martin DeHaan (editor of Our Daily Bread – a devotional booklet published by Radio Bible Class) told of a time when he had used the slate to draw a horrible picture of the teacher. Just then the teacher came walking towards him. Quickly he grabbed the moist sponge hanging beside his desk to erase what was on the slate. The evidence was gone in one swoosh of the sponge. How he loved that sponge.

There is an even better eraser. Did you know that, according to scripture, God can and does have a record of every word, action and even the thoughts of our minds? (Psalm 139:1-4) We can't remove them. But the grace of God offers us an opportunity to wipe away the record of our negative words, deeds and thoughts. Isaiah wrote that though your sins be as scarlet, they shall be as white as snow. The slate can be wiped clean because Jesus death on the cross has paid for that to be possible. That is an act of grace: getting something good when we deserved something bad. It's available.

We should be very grateful for grace.

FLEEING THE CONGO

A young man named Safari was fleeing the civil war raging in the Congo. A person he knew, Gilbert, had just murdered Safari's parents. We can imagine that Safari must have fled in fear, resorted to hiding, then was plagued by weariness and deprivation as he sought to cope with the circumstances. He finally arrived at the Dzaleka refugee camp in Malawi after four months on foot. In the camp there were still undercurrents of ethnic tensions. Rather than withdraw from the situation Safari felt called to start meeting with people willing to listen to the message of the gospel of peace and reconciliation. Many were ready for that, and soon a rudimentary church was planted (not a building). Recently, Randy Friesen visited that camp in Malawi.

Safari must have been more than just surprised two years later. Who should come into the refugee camp but Gilbert, the murderer? He was no longer a militia leader but a fleeing refugee himself. Rather than seek revenge Safari lived up to his commitment to peace and reconciliation. He connected with him, invited him to a meal and then invited him to stay in his home. That lasted three years. Over time this consistent expression of unbelievable kindness convinced Gilbert to become a follower of Christ too. He now works alongside Safari to minister to a network of 36 church groups enrolling about 11,000 believers! This truly is faith in action as it was meant to be.

Reported by Randy Friesen, in the Mennonite
Brethren Witness magazine, Summer, 2019

DEBT PAID IN FULL

A wealthy nobleman was out for a late night stroll when he noticed a light still shining in the front room of his nephew's home. A closer look revealed that he was slumped on to the table. Somewhat concerned, since his nephew was living alone, he walked to the front door and tested it. It was unlocked so he quietly went in. A closer look at his nephew from the door confirmed that he was alive, just sleeping. But the sight of a revolver near his outstretched hand on the table struck fear in his heart. On the other side was a note. Stealthily getting closer he looked at the note in full view on the table. The words on it were grim.

It's hopeless. There's no way out of this debt.

Strewn over the rest of the table were several bills, large ones, unwise ones and some with severe warnings. The man leaned over the table and wrote across his nephew's note: **Paid In Full!!** He also signed his name. Then he gathered up the bills plus the revolver and left.

Minutes later the nephew awoke with a start. His gun and the bills were missing. Across his note he read the marvelous news. He could hardly believe what he saw! Now there was hope and the chance of a new life.

We have also amassed an insurmountable debt of sin against God. The crucifixion was all about offering a Paid in Full receipt, compliments of His Son, Jesus. The resurrection confirmed that the payment was adequate. It's free to us but obtained at a high price. The chorus of a song shares this wonderful news:

> *He paid a debt He did not owe, I owed a debt I could not pay,*
> *I needed Someone to wash my sins away.*
> *And now I sing a brand new song, Amazing Grace, the whole day long.*
> *Christ Jesus paid the debt that I could never pay.*

DELETE BUTTON

Did you know that guilt can be erased? It would be pointless for me to think I can avoid guilt because God knows and can record every word I've ever said, everything I've ever done and even every thought I've ever had.

Ps. 139:1-4 *"You have searched me, LORD, and you know me. You know when I sit and when I rise; you perceive my thoughts from afar. You discern my going out and my lying down; you are familiar with all my ways. Before a word is on my tongue you, LORD, know it completely."*

The good news is that an unbelievably fabulous deal is available! God has a delete button! He would love to erase it all but it is not an automatic action. It is His choice that both His love and His holiness, His compassion and His justice, must be satisfied. He therefore has arranged for Jesus to take upon Himself the whole debt load for everyone on earth by dying on the cross for us as payment. Forgiveness is available to everyone who acknowledges accountability to God, admits sinfulness as the wrong way to live and asks for mercy. The thieving tax collector in Luke 18 prayed, *"God be merciful to me sinner."* That met those basic requirements God was looking for and the tax collector went away justified, forgiven. The Pharisee who was boasting about how good he was did not leave justified.

For the repentant tax collector God pressed the delete button, for the proud Pharisee, not. We have the same choice. I can appear before God with my debt paid in full or bear the consequences myself.

Incredible opportunity!!

DISCONNECTED

Our 9 year old grandson came to me with a battery operated toy car that wasn't working. After several efforts to make it work I gave up and informed him that, since it was only a cheap item, he might as well throw it away. But Timmy didn't give up. He went away with the car, took it apart and found a loose wire in the mechanism.

When he brought it back to me we inserted batteries that we knew were good and behold, it worked!

We sometimes treat others, and ourselves, that way. We look at someone who is really down and see them as disposable junk, not worth trying to fix. We get depressed about our own state and conclude that we are not worth keeping either. Jesus met a number of people like that but He found the loose wire, the disconnection. He was derided as the friend of despised tax collectors and sinners, even befriending prostitutes. He had a way of getting inside and identifying what was broken. Better still, He could make them whole. He still invites people in the words of Matthew 11:28 *"Come to Me, all you who are weary and burdened, and I will give you rest."*

There's room for you on the sunny side.

DUTCH ELM BEETLE

For decades the tree withstood storms and hardships of every kind. Gale force winds, lightning strikes, freezing rain that coated it with ice and even a fire had all threatened to bring it down, but the elm stood strong. But one summer its leaves shriveled and died before the fall came. Its limbs became gaunt and lifeless. What had happened? Inspection revealed the infection of Dutch Elm beetles. These tiny creatures brought down the mighty elm which had survived the onslaught of fierce attacks by bigger foes. What is this saying to me?

I could weather the temptations to steal, commit adultery, murder, plot a violent revenge, or hatch a shady business deal but miss the less obvious pitfalls. If I allow hidden resentments to fester, secret pride to discredit me, or harbor illicit sexual fantasies they may cause my downfall when storms couldn't. Integrity and trust are priceless.

But there is good news, very good news! The Lord offers to pay the debt for all of those and set us free. If we acknowledge Him, admit our need as sinners and ask for forgiveness He will wash them all away, help us to live right and welcome us home at the end of life.

FORGIVENESS

Forgiveness is something we all need to both give and receive. The consequences of harboring unforgiveness, or not being willing to accept forgiveness, are severe. Some people have great difficulty with this thought because they have the wrong idea about what forgiveness is.

Forgiveness is NOT pretending that the affront never happened.

Forgiveness is NOT saying that I wasn't really hurt by the event.

Forgiveness is NOT releasing the offender from all consequences of the error.

But forgiveness is refusing to nurse the grudge and thereby allowing it to continue hurting you. It is letting go of the resentment and allowing God (or sometimes governing authorities) to deal with it. It is refusing to hang onto demands for 'payment' from the offender until that person comes with an apology or recompense. They still need to come, but you are not allowing it to keep on hurting you by dwelling on it.

As someone has succinctly stated: *"Unforgiveness is like drinking poison and hoping the other person will die."*

The biggest incentive to forgive comes with the realization that God offers full forgiveness for all we have done, which is far more than what others have done to us.

Forgive!

GOD'S GRACE

George Thomas, pastor in a small New England town, one Sunday morning came to the church service carrying a rusty, bent, old bird cage, and set it by the pulpit. Eyebrows were raised and, as if in response, Pastor Thomas began to speak.

"I was walking through town yesterday when I saw a young boy coming toward me swinging this bird cage. On the bottom of the cage were three little wild birds, shivering with cold and fright. I stopped the lad and asked, "What do you have there, son?"

"Just some old birds," came the reply.

"What are you going to do with them?" I asked.

"Take 'em home and have fun with 'em," he answered. "I'm gonna tease 'em and pull out their feathers to make 'em fight. I'm gonna have a real good time."

"But you'll get tired of those birds sooner or later. What will you do then?"

"Oh, I got some cats," said the little boy. "They like birds. I'll take 'em to them."

The pastor was silent for a moment. "How much do you want for those birds, son?"

"Huh?? !!! Why, you don't want them birds, mister. They're just plain old field birds. They don't sing. They ain't even pretty!"

"How much?" the pastor asked again. The boy sized up the pastor as if he were crazy and said, "$10?"

The pastor reached into his pocket and took out a ten dollar bill. He placed it in the boy's hand. In a flash, the boy was gone. The pastor picked up the cage and gently carried it to the end of the alley where there was a tree and a grassy spot. Setting the cage down, he opened the door, and by softly tapping the bars persuaded the birds out, setting them free.

In a similar way Satan has trapped many people, gloating over the sinister fun he will have with them. For a while the cage may seem to give provision and protection but Satan's goal is to generate hatred, abuse, cursing, killing and resentment. Then he would like to achieve his ultimate goal, death for them, but Jesus has intervened. He came to pay the price for their redemption. It cost Him His life blood for a world of people who didn't appreciate what He came to do. They spit on Him, cursed Him and killed Him, but He used that very action to bring about the plan of salvation. That offer of salvation is available to all who acknowledge their accountability to God, admit they are sinners and ask for mercy. In Luke 18:9 – 14 the despised tax collector prayed, "God, have mercy on me a sinner." The Lord declared that he left the temple justified, forgiven. You too can be freed from this trap in the same way.

At this point Pastor Thomas picked up the cage and walked out.

VIEW FROM SPACE

While driving home from Osoyoos to Oliver, BC, a few years ago I listened to an interview with Chris Hadfield, speaking from the International Space Station. He commented on how beautiful planet earth looked, how terrible it was to imagine the devastation in so many war-torn, impoverished areas. It hurt to think of how much people need to learn how to get along, care for the planet and then enjoy life.

Most religions, philosophies, ideologies and belief systems try to address such issues. The astronaut's personal convictions were not declared but the general consensus amongst the public seems to be that we should each have a belief system, keep it to ourselves, respect other beliefs and just get on with a life that cares for others and cares for the environment. Mankind has never accomplished that, but there is hope, there is a solution.

There is Someone Else looking down at planet earth. He is the Creator and Owner with a definite plan of His own and advice about what is real, true and important. God created the universe for a purpose. Although sin has marred that goal, the good news is that God knows how to fix it. He pays the penalty Himself in the Person of Christ, granting forgiveness freely to all who call on Him.

"Call upon Me in the day of trouble. I will deliver you and you shall glorify Me." Psalm 50:15

ICEBERGS

From a distance icebergs are impressive, even beautiful. Up close they can be dangerous. Most of the iceberg, 90% they say, is hidden below the water line. To approach closely is to risk serious or even fatal damage to the ship's hull.

Are we that way more often than we'd like to admit? We have our public image, our outward appearance that looks good to others. But when they rub into us up close it's another matter. What we've been harboring inside comes into play. Warmth, hospitality and flexibility are not the attributes of an iceberg.

Jesus had severe words for those who pretended to be one thing but inside were something very different. He said, *"Everything they do is done for men to see." Matthew 23:5.* We are adept at trying to make ourselves look good but is it only external or superficial?

What is the issue that causes us to do that? We are in it for ourselves, not the Lord and not for others. We don't have the priority of honoring the Lord but strive to enhance our own image. I know that from personal experience. This is directly opposite to what Jesus taught as the two most important priorities. They are: *"Love the Lord your God* (that's first) and *love your neighbor as yourself."* (That comes second.) See Mark 12:30 – 31.

That melts the iceberg and turns it into life giving fresh water in the midst of undrinkable ocean water. For the iceberg the fresh water is soon lost in the sea. We don't have to let that happen to our attitude in our community. This transformation can happen as we place our faith in the Lord to forgive our sins and make us a new person.

KIM PHUC, THE NAPALM GIRL

Nine year old Phan Thi Kim Phuc and 30 others were hiding in the temple of Trang Bang, South Vietnam. It was the summer of 1972. Enemy soldiers were threatening to shoot them if they were found. Suddenly there was a new threat, bombs in canisters of napalm that would burn down the temple. Run!! As they fled one canister exploded just behind Kim, burning her clothes. With skin peeling off her back and left arm she ran down the street naked and screaming. Photographer Nick Ut's picture of her running and screaming shocked the world. Nearby journalists poured water over her body and took her to the local hospital, where she was put into the morgue. Hopeless case. She won't survive.

Three days after the raid Captain John Plummer saw that picture in a military newspaper. He had double-checked with informed personnel to confirm that there were no villagers left who would be endangered by the bombing raid he was to order. A nightmare of guilt swept over him and stretched into nearly 24 years of regret. It cost him his marriage and drove him to drink as he kept his involvement as much a secret as he could.

Kim's mother found her alive in the morgue and rescued her. Kim endured fourteen months of agony during 17 skin grafts. This was followed by years of painful recovery. There were times of bitter resentment. Meanwhile, Kim was pursuing a medical career where she hoped to help others as she had been helped. A casual reading of a New Testament confronted her with the claim that Jesus was the Way, the Truth and the Life. It also presented the idea that bitterness is too heavy a burden, she needed to forgive the bomber. The account of Jesus offering forgiveness to the soldiers who crucified Him convinced her to believe in Jesus. Her government sent her to Cuba for courses in pharmacology. There she met and married Bui Hay Toan. Returning from a honeymoon in Moscow, the plane landed for refueling in Gander, Newfoundland. The two of them went to the immigration officer instead of re-boarding the plane. The future looked better.

John Plummer battled depression, guilt and alcoholism until he met and married Joanne, who helped him recover from alcoholism. John became a Christian and at age 47 was ordained as a Methodist minister. But one key issue remained to be settled. He longed to meet Kim and seek forgiveness so that he could become free of recurring nightmares. How could he ever find her? Maybe she's not even alive?

In June, 1996, Plummer spotted that picture of the napalm girl in a newscast which stated that she was now 33 and living in Toronto. She was scheduled to speak at the Vietnam Veteran's Memorial in Washington, D.C. on Nov. 11, 1996. This would be his chance. Traveling from Purcellville, Virginia, he heard her say to the crowd,

"If I could talk face to face with the pilot who dropped the bombs, I could tell him we cannot change history, but we should try to do good things for the future." He wanted to talk to her but his one chance seemed to be slipping away as Kim was being led away. John Plummer jumped the dividing rope and managed to get her attention and explain his reason for being there. He could only say, "I'm sorry. I am so sorry." Kim responded, "It's OK. I forgive." Kim hugged a tearful John Plummer as finally his nightmare was over.

Forgiveness moves you from the dark side to the sunny side.

Based on a November, 1997 article in the
Reader's digest plus internet sources.

LOVE BROKE HIS HEART

George W. Truett, pastor of First Baptist in Dallas from 1897 until his death in 1944, conducted a mission Sunday School in the town where he lived prior to his Dallas pastorate. One ten year old boy in that Sunday School was accidentally shot by a neighbor's boy. It was serious. Two doctors arrived to help the lad but they concluded that there was little hope of saving his life. The father was in his usual drunken stupor and was of no help. The next day George Truett returned to the home and found the boy still alive and the father sober but in tears.

"Son, you'll soon get well," the father sobbed.

The child feebly whispered, "No, papa, I won't be getting well."

"You'll get well and I'll become a good father," the man insisted.

Between gasps for breath the child murmured, "When I am gone, papa, I want you to remember that I loved you even if you did get drunk and angry."

The boy died. But what the scoldings and criticisms of the neighbors over the years had not achieved, this son's declaration of love did. It broke the father's heart. That was enough to cause him to turn to the Lord and keep his promise of a drastic lifestyle change.

WHITE FACE

One story that, for a while, dominated the news in 2019 reminded me of an eye-opening experience I had in Kenya, but it was about whiteface. My wife and I enlisted for one year of voluntary service at the Kijabe Mission station. The commitment was for '92-'93. I was teaching at Moffat Bible College and Helen helped out with some clerical work at the Administration Office.

One of the expectations from some students was that the teacher would conduct an evangelistic outreach in their villages, preach in their churches and visit their families. When Peter Ngya asked me to come with him to Karuri for that purpose I readily agreed. I was frequently gone to such places over the weekend, sometimes Helen accompanied me. I was a bit puzzled when Peter told me, in an apologetic sort of way, that the church leadership agreed to this invitation. I thought to myself, "Why would he express it that way? Of course the leadership has to be in favor. Is there something more to this?"

I was billeted in the home of the chairman of the board. During the evening of my arrival the pastor and a group of others came to the home, welcomed me and were gracious hosts. The conversation soon revealed that both the pastor and the chairman had been jailed for being part of a revolt against British colonial domination over 30 years ago. In fact, extremists in the Mau Mau movement adopted the slogan, "Kill the white man!" Resentments had run deep. Foreigners were grabbing more and more of the best land and reducing Kenyans to poorly paid laborers. At one point about 17,000 Europeans owned

48,000 square kilometers of the best Kikuyu land while over a million Kikuyu tribespeople were allotted 18,000 square kilometers. This fueled the resentment and sparked massive rallies in protest. The colonial government responded to the revolt by banning all public gatherings except for church services. No problem, vowed the movement. We'll form a church and continue meeting. They called their denomination the Africa Independent Pentecostal Church of Africa. It was a front for their political agenda. When the colonial government discovered this they expropriated this church's property and gave it to other organizations including some supposed church missions but the Africa Inland Mission, now centered in Kijabe, opposed that idea and did not accept such property. The ensuing war claimed the lives of an estimated 100,000 – 300,000 Kenyans over the 1920-1963 period. In addition the colonial government executed more than 1000 of the revolt's leaders. *(Check the details on Wikipedia.)*

When independence was finally achieved in 1963 the AIPCA lost its initial mandate and changed its slogan to "No white people allowed in our churches." I was told just before the Sunday service that the pulpit had been moved off the platform and onto the main floor. I thought nothing of it, no problem. It was a concession to an element in the congregation still angry with the white man. The platform was occupied by an array of leaders in various clerical robes. Obviously the white man didn't belong among them and I was very content with that.

After the service a number of speeches were made. Peter told me he'd explain later. It turned out that they were speeches about reconciliation with the white man and the need for forgiveness and putting the past behind them. Peter told me that I was the first white man to preach in this church (but not from the platform, yet). My face was the wrong color. I carry no credit for this small breakthrough, since I was clueless about what was happening, but give credit to the Lord and them for the step they did take.

THEME 8

Goals

Am I expected to have goals for my life?

"And this is my prayer: that your love may abound more and more in knowledge and depth of insight, so that you may be able to discern what is best and may be pure and blameless for the day of Christ, filled with the fruit of righteousness that comes through Jesus Christ--to the glory and praise of God." Philippians 1:9-11

CHILD OF THE KING

Many have dreamed of being part of a royal family. They imagine how fantastically great that would be. Now the talk has been about the line-up for the throne in England. The current queen, in spite of many challenges and not being faultless, has been a positive example of what a committed monarch should be like. Singing *"God Save the Queen"* may well have significant meaning. Although the media may convey a picture of delight for royalty, this sentiment isn't always the reality.

Harriett Buell was walking home from a Sunday morning church service one day when kings must have been mentioned. Thoughts about life in a royal family must have been running through her mind. What would that be like? Then she realized that she already was in an even better royal family. As part of the family of God she already was a child of the King! She was so taken by the thought that upon reaching home she wrote a poem that included these words.

> *My Father is rich in houses and lands, He holds the wealth of the world in His hands.*
>
> *Of rubies and diamonds, of silver and gold. His coffers are full — He has riches untold.*
>
> *A tent or a cottage, why should I care? They're building a palace for me over there!*
>
> *Though exiled from home, yet still I may sing: All glory to God, I'm a child of the King!*

It's even brighter up ahead.

CORE VALUES

What would you choose as the three most important core values in life? A core value is more than just a good character trait. It identifies essential principles on how to live life, or how to manage a home, or what the central aims of an organization should be. Admittedly, they are most often idealistic but still good to have.

Reflecting back on the many years behind me, studying life, pondering the many mistakes and failures and also some successes, I have come to the following conclusion. The three principles I would choose can be summarized as achievement, affirmation and affection. Without these life becomes meaningless.

Achievement is not found only in high academic marks. Each person can be good at something. To find and develop that skill is to have found your niche. We make a big mistake if the only standard is getting A's and B's in a school report card. (I was a school principal for 15 years.) The list of possible achievements is very long.

Affirmation says that the person is valued for who he/she is, not just by what they've done. We are a wonderful, complex creation in the image of God. He doesn't make junk. But handled poorly we might devalue ourselves and others.

Affection is love. Love does not mean giving someone everything and anything they want. It is doing what's best for that person. Caring about others must rank as one of the highest achievements.

There we have it! Triple AAA core values. Impossible to live up to on our own but by grace through faith in the One who made us we will grow in that ability.

EMPTY HOPE

"If we could sniff or swallow something that would, for five or six hours each day, abolish our solitude as individuals, atone us with our fellows in a glowing exaltation of affection and make life in all its aspects seem

not only worth living, but divinely beautiful and significant, and if this heavenly, world-transfiguring drug were of such a kind that we could wake up next morning with a clear head and an undamaged constitution-then, it seems to me, all our problems (and not merely the one small problem of discovering a novel pleasure) would be wholly solved and earth would become paradise." Aldous Huxley

"Two thousand pharmacologists and bio-chemists were subsidized. Six years later it was being produced commercially. The perfect drug. Euphoric, narcotic, pleasantly hallucinant. All the advantages of Christianity and alcohol; none of their defects. Take a holiday from reality whenever you like, and come back without so much as a headache or a mythology. Stability was practically assured." Aldous Huxley (*Brave New World*)

"A world of genetically modified babies, boundless consumption, casual sex and drugs… How does Aldous Huxley's vision of a totalitarian future stand up 75 years after Brave New World was first published?" Margaret Atwood

Reality check?

LOST OPPORTUNITY

Mark Twain, the author, was approached by a man who wanted him to invest in a project he was pursuing. Twain listened for a while but then shook his head, saying, "I can't afford to do that. I've been burned too often. I can't risk putting any more money into someone else's plan." "But this will benefit society and change the world," the man argued. "No, I won't invest," asserted Twain. As the man was walking away Mark Twain called after him, "What did you say your name was?" "Bell," the man answered, "Alexander Graham Bell." The project: telephone.

Source: May 5, 1963 devotional item in Our Daily Bread, published by Radio Bible Class.

Later on Twain realized that he had missed a great opportunity. However, missing an opportunity to gain a chunk of money isn't nearly as bad as missing opportunities to encourage or build up other people who really need a positive touch. In the days ahead there will be opportunities to encourage, uplift and cheer up some people. Though we can't be expected to respond every time, yet we may just be in the right place to do that for somebody. Can you think of a time when you were encouraged by something someone said or did? Pay it forward. Let's not miss our opportunities.

PLEASURE CENTER

Recently scientists have identified a 'pleasure center' in the brain which can be stimulated directly. Researchers have implanted electrodes in the hypothalamuses of rats, who are then placed in a cage in front of three levers. Pressing the first releases a piece of food, the second lever yields a drink, and the third activates electrodes that give the rats an immediate but transient feeling of pleasure. Laboratory rats quickly figure out the three levers, and in these experiments the rats chose to press only the pleasure lever, day after day, until they starve to death. Why respond to hunger and thirst when they can enjoy the pleasures associated with eating and drinking in a more convenient way?

From *Gift of Pain* by Philip Yancy and Dr. Paul Brand p. 297

We may be inclined to ridicule those misguided rats but do we as human beings do something similar at times? Whether it is in minor ways that have small consequences or serious addictions that cause huge problems, we may keep doing the harmful things that give immediate satisfaction without considering the long term disastrous results.

There is a bright side to all this. We can substitute a positive pursuit for this damaging one. And the Lord would love to help us do that.

OPTIONS

Many people who want to find some meaning in life pursue one of four options: fun and games (pleasure); money and things (possessions); influence and control (power); or recognition and achievement (prestige). We all need a measure of each one of these. There are essential, positive benefits to be had from them. The problem comes if even one of them becomes the number one priority. Unbalanced obsession has caused huge damage to relationships. Most of us either know someone personally, or know about someone, who has met with disastrous results by pursuing unrestrained pleasure, or greed for money, or grasped for power over people, or was consumed by the pride of personal achievements. None of their stories ended well.

The answer that Jesus gave to one who questioned him about what was most important seems like such a simple and reasonable solution. First, love God; then love people as much as you love yourself. Easy to say, tough to do, but wouldn't that move us into the sunny side?

REFLECTIONS

As I reflect on the more than 24 years we lived in Oliver, BC, before moving to Chilliwack, BC, I think of so many experiences that have brought joy and wonder, so many friends and acquaintances we have come to know, so many mistakes I've made that caused grief and have taught me lessons, but also many great and enjoyable events that have provided good memories. Many are the funerals and memorials that I've conducted or attended as well as joyful weddings and social events. It's overwhelming! Put together they remind me that:

- inheritance may be a material thing or money we give **to** someone;
- memories are impressions, good or bad, that we leave **with** someone;

- but a legacy is the difference, positive or negative, that we make **in** someone.

As the Dolly Parton trio song says:

When we're gone, long gone, the only thing that will have mattered is the love that we shared and the way that we cared, when we're gone, long gone.

May what we leave behind draw someone to the sunny side.

REMARKABLE ANSWERS

Helen and I had been searching for about two years to find a Care Facility setting that would accommodate Helen's needs in her advancing stages of Parkinson's. Her list of hopes, requests and prayers were very specific:

- a community of buildings that housed all three major levels of care,
- built and operated by a Christian society,
- near to family and friends,
- attractively landscaped and away from downtown,
- near a park or river and somewhat removed from congestion.

This amounted to a half-way house to heaven!! I thought she was asking for too much. We searched up and down the Okanagan and some Care Facilities fulfilled part of the list. We put our names on a waiting list for one of them. While we were in Chilliwack for our granddaughter's wedding, a friend mentioned that the Elim Society was building a Village on 9.5 acres near the Vedder River that just might fit. We checked it out. It is developed and operated by the Elim Society, a Christian group that has very successfully built and operated a 20 acre Village in Surrey. The first independent living building is now ready, with buildings to follow that will house supportive and residential care levels. We both have many family members, relatives and friends in Chilliwack and Abbotsford. The only two-bedroom units unclaimed were on the first floor. We put our claim in for a unit.

On the way back to Oliver Helen said that it would be nice if:

- we could have a corner unit instead of one sandwiched between two other units,
- the windows in that unit faced east and south to combat SADS,
- that unit would be on the second or third floor for greater security and privacy.

Now she was asking for a place three quarters of the way to heaven!

We were supposed to come back on Sept. 29 to finalize matters but it was post-poned to Oct. 6 due to circumstances beyond their control. After we met with the Elim financial representative on Oct. 6 to sign for the unit I just thought I'd ask, at the end, if any two-bedroom units on the 2nd or 3rd floor had been relinquished. "Yes", she said. "One just became available a few hours ago." Helen asked, "Is it a corner unit?" Yes, it was! "Do the windows face south and east?" Yes, they did. We marvelled at the realization that every one of the 8 specific requests were answered. Had we come on the Sept. 29th date, the corner unit would not have been available.

Thank you, Lord! You've been good to us far beyond what we deserve, even though our biggest request, for Helen's healing, has not been answered yet. It isn't about what we are going through that really counts, but how we go through it.

RESERVATIONS

Making reservations is a common event. We reserve a flight, a motel room, a restaurant meal, a tee time for golf, a seat for the concert and many other things. Did you know that God is open for reservations too? It wouldn't be a good idea to just show up at a cruise ship and expect to have a place available. But God says He will have a place for those who come. John 6:37 *"All that the Father gives me will come to me, and whoever comes to me I will never drive away."*

A. When we make a reservation here on earth we will be asked, "And how will you be paying for this?" Reserving a place with the Lord after this life is over is **free** but **not cheap.** Jesus says that He'll pay for it with His own blood. 1 Corinthians 6:20 *"You were bought at a price."*

B. What are the things He'll reserve for us?

1. He'll reserve a remarkable flight for you. 1 Thessalonians 4:16-17 *"For the Lord himself will come down from heaven, with a loud command, with the voice of the archangel and with the trumpet call of God, and the dead in Christ will rise first. After that, we who are still alive and are left will be caught up together with them in the clouds to meet the Lord in the air. And so we will be with the Lord forever."*

2. He'll reserve a room for you. *John 14:2 "In my Father's house are many rooms; if it were not so, I would have told you. I am going there to prepare a place for you."*

3. He'll reserve a seat for you at His banquet. *Revelations 19:9 "Blessed are those who are invited to the wedding supper of the Lamb!"*

C. How do you make such a reservation? The story of the tax collector and the Pharisee in Luke 18:10-14 tells us that when the tax collector prayed, *"God have mercy on me a sinner"*, He left that place justified. He had made his reservation. He acknowledged God, admitted his sin, and asked for mercy. It was a triple A plan: acknowledge, admit, ask. Have you made your reservation?

SHORT CUTS

Have you ever taken a short cut, only to find yourself in big trouble? A map may have shown the route to be one mile shorter but it took 45 minutes longer due to the condition of the road. Often the road you know is better than the way you don't know.

My wife and I were in Kenya, Africa for a year of voluntary service (1992-93) with the Africa Inland Mission. I remember taking a carload of African students to help out at an orphanage. On the way there, a short cut was available instead of taking the longer route on pavement. What a mistake that was! We became stuck in mud. The mud and water under the car got into the engine and even into the rotary distributor (remember those?). This was about 26 years ago. When I took the distributor cap off to clean the contacts, I inadvertently dropped the contact piece that carried the electric spark. In the mud and the oncoming darkness it was fruitless to search for it. Night was coming. We were in a somewhat remote, wild animal territory. What now? A light in the distance indicated a home was not far away. The owner came as requested and suggested extracting the core from a flashlight battery to fashion a replacement contact. It worked! With students pushing and I at the wheel we made it out of the mud and then on to the orphanage. Praise the Lord for a timely rescue!!

So much for short cuts. They are even more damaging when it comes to the quality of workmanship or integrity in relationships.

SNOW PLOW

It was snowing heavily. The driver was very insecure because the visibility was so low. Remembering the following advice: *"If you spot a snow plow during a heavy snowfall when you're driving in an unfamiliar place, just get behind it and follow"*, the driver was relieved to spot one and moved into place behind the plow. After about ten minutes the driver of the plow stopped and came to the car.

"Is something the matter? Are you alright?" asked the snow plow operator.

"Yes, I'm OK. Is there a problem?"

"No, but you need to know that I've finished the Walmart parking lot and am now going down the street to do the Safeway lot."

Not every bit of advice you get will take you to your goal.

SURPRISED

I was part of a team from our church that conducted church services in three different Care Facilities. We took our turn along with other teams from a number of churches. I was drawn to the topic of heaven as I prepared for one service at Sunnybank a while ago. In the group that assembled was a man who was wheeled in on a recliner that actually folded back into something like a bed. I did not recognize the person and he seemed unresponsive. We sang and spoke and prayed about the great prospect that lies before us. After it was over I tried to have a word with each one who had attended. The man on the stretcher turned out to be Pastor Peter Neave from Park Drive Church, who himself had been conducting such services for years, and whom I knew personally. He was unable to communicate clearly but I could tell that he knew who I was.

A few days later I came back for a visit with him and found him alert and talkative. He mentioned how much he appreciated the thoughts shared about heaven on the previous Wednesday. The one who I thought was completely out of it with no idea of what was going on was the one to whom it meant the most. A few days later Peter died. Now he was personally experiencing what we could only talk about.

There are surprises along the sunny road of life.

WOMAN AND A FORK

A young woman, (some versions say Mrs. Smith) who had been diagnosed with a terminal illness, had been given three months to live. So, as she was getting her things in order, she contacted her pastor (some versions say Pastor Phillip) and had him come to her house to discuss certain aspects of her final wishes. She told him which songs she wanted sung at the service, what scriptures she would like read, and what outfit she wanted to be buried in.

Everything was in order and the pastor was preparing to leave when the young woman suddenly remembered something very important to her. "There's one more thing," she said excitedly. "What's that?" was the pastor's request. "This is very important," the young woman continued. "I want to be buried with a fork in my right hand." The pastor stood looking at the young woman, not knowing quite what to say. "That surprises you, doesn't it," the young woman declared. "Well, to be honest, I'm puzzled by the request," said the pastor.

"In all my years of attending socials and dinners, I always remember that when the dishes of the main course were being cleared, someone would inevitably lean over and say, '**Keep your fork.**' It was my favorite part because I knew that something better was coming, like velvety chocolate cake or deep-dish apple pie. Something wonderful, and with substance! So, I just want people to see me there in that casket with a fork in my hand and I want them to wonder: What's with the fork?" Then I want you to tell them: "**Keep your fork, the best is yet to come.**"

Roger W. Thomas, 1994

WORLDVIEW

In early January, 2013, I was listening to the car radio as Astronaut Chris Hadfield spoke about his experiences in space while circling far above us in the International Space Station. Among other comments he spoke about how distressing it was for him to look at planet earth as a beautiful blue-green sight while at the same time knowing that war, violence, poverty and crime were making life horrible for millions. If only people would give priority to those things that are real, true and important, we could live in peace and harmony.

A person's conclusions about what is real, true and important have been called that person's worldview. We all have a worldview of some sort whether we realize it or not. For some it is well-defined, for some rather vague. A major problem is that some can articulate a very commendable and admirable worldview in words, but deny it by their actions.

Theists

Chris Hadfield isn't the only one who has looked down on planet earth and wondered about the people on it.

2Chronicles 16:9 *"For the eyes of the LORD range throughout the earth to strengthen those whose hearts are fully committed to him."*

1Peter 3:12 *"For the eyes of the Lord are on the righteous and his ears are attentive to their prayer, but the face of the Lord is against those who do evil."*

There are 88 verses in Scripture that speak of the eyes of the Lord assessing people on planet earth. These people are made in His image according to His purposes. The Lord's statement on what is real, true and important for them is based on what He stands for. Those who identify with that are **theists.**

Religionists

In contrast there are those who prefer to manufacture a god in man's image instead of God making us in His image. This home-made deity and man-made belief system becomes a replacement religion.

Psalm 4:2 *"How long, O men, will you turn my glory into shame? How long will you love delusions and seek false gods?"*

Romans 10:3 *"Since they did not know the righteousness that comes from God and sought to establish their own, they did not submit to God's righteousness."*

These people could be called **religionists**.

Humanists

A third group are the ones who reject the idea of any god existing or at least live as though God didn't exist or count. They form a worldview from a totally human perspective. It leaves God out. We'll do things by ourselves, are accountable only to ourselves and will set the standards ourselves.

Job 8:13 *"Such is the destiny of all who forget God; so perishes the hope of the godless."*

Hosea 4:1 *"…the LORD has a charge to bring against you who live in the land: "There is no faithfulness, no love, no acknowledgment of God in the land."*

These are the **humanists**.

Narcistic hedonists

These people prefer not to think about belief systems, standards, morality or accountability. They love pleasure and themselves too much to be bothered. Their self-indulgent and self-centered lifestyle leaves no room for such thoughts.

2 Timothy 3:2-5 *"People will be lovers of themselves, lovers of money, boastful, proud, abusive, disobedient to their parents, ungrateful, unholy, without love, unforgiving, slanderous, without self-control, brutal, not lovers of the good, treacherous, rash, conceited, lovers of pleasure rather than lovers of God—having a form of godliness but denying its power. Have nothing to do with them."*

These are **narcistic hedonists.**

Application

It's time to assess our own position in all of this. Remember that it isn't what I say is my worldview, my actions will identify it. How can we get an objective view of what that may be? Five questions will help. I call them the W5 questions: who, what, when, where and why.

1. Where did we and everything around us come from?
2. Why are we here?
3. What went wrong?
4. Who will fix it?
5. When we die what happens to us?

An honest answer to each of these questions will tell us what is real, important and true in our belief system.

THEME 9

Special Days

Is it important to observe, even celebrate, special days?

"Let's have a feast and celebrate." Luke 15:23

DADDY, ARE YOU THERE?

A wee voice from the nighttime called, "Daddy, are you there?
Is your face turned toward me? If it is I will not care
that the night is dark and fearsome – I'll just go to sleep again."
And the voice trailed off in slumber with never a care or pain.

And we who are growing older, as we lay ourselves to rest,
with minds that are distracted and hearts with cares oppressed.
We can still be brave in darkness, and know our Father's near.
With His face turned toward us we can sleep without a fear.

Composed by A.D. Martin over 50 years ago.

Fathers, you are very important to your children.

CELEBRATION

On July 1 we celebrate the anniversary of the formation of Canada. It's good to celebrate that. Even though Canada would be considered a youngster on the world scene I believe we are one of the best countries to live in. We are very fortunate!

Do the angels and God ever celebrate anything? It doesn't take long to realize that they certainly have and will continue to do so.

According to Job 38:4-7 and Psalm 8 they celebrated the creation of the universe. Ours is an incredibly marvelous and complex planet.

The 15th chapter of Luke tells us that the angels have a party when someone turns to the Lord in repentance. It is cause for rejoicing.

A huge choir of angels announced the birth of Jesus in Bethlehem according to Luke chapter two. No other baby has equalled that welcome even though each one has been very special.

It was also angels who made a point of showing up at the empty tomb of Jesus on the morning of His resurrection. We are told in the New Testament that without the resurrection of Christ our faith is in vain. They were undoubtedly exuberant about this astounding event.

We have lots of reasons to celebrate along with them.

THANKSGIVING OR COMPLAINING?

Do we have something to complain about? It has been claimed that many (not all) of our ancestors did without the following:

- without sugar in many places before the 13th century;
- without coal fires until the 14th century;
- without buttered bread until the 15th century;
- without potatoes until the 16th century;
- without coffee, tea or soap until the 17th century;
- without pudding until the 18th century;
- without gas, matches or electricity until the 19th century; and
- without canned goods until the 20th century.

Add to that all the conveniences, inventions, gadgets, electronics, vehicles and much more that we have today and are we still not content? We haven't yet even mentioned the love of God and the wonderful creation He has made for us!

Now, what was that we were complaining about? Worth considering more often than just on Thanksgiving weekend!

FATHER'S DAY

"One father is worth more than a hundred schoolmasters."
--17th Century English Proverb

Father's Day has a special message just for dads. Thank you for being there for your family!

Marvelous things occur because of you being a part of your children's lives.

You are their role model, counselor, teacher and the source of strength that your family needs and enjoys. Your importance in the lives of your children can immediately be seen in their eyes and actions. Your time and involvement with your children creates an influence that can't be measured. Dads have the opportunity to do that. For example, there is an overwhelming amount of data from social research that tells a pretty impressive story.

For one thing, if you are there and involved, those children are 50% more likely to do well in high school and go on to college. Not only that, but just by having you around and being supportive, your children are over 60% less likely to get into trouble or see the inside of a juvenile detention hall.

And what about your precious daughters? Well, if you are not around and involved, your daughters are twice as likely to become sexually involved at a young age and they have a 70% higher chance of getting pregnant outside of marriage. The list of positive things that you bring into your children's lives is long. It is clear, you can make a big difference.

FATHER'S DAY

How did Father's Day come to be recognized in so many countries? According to Wikipedia and other sources, several persons have claimed to be its founder. However, the initiative that is most widely accepted as successful is the following one.

Sonora Smart Dodd was the daughter of the civil war veteran William Jackson Smart. He raised six children as a single parent after his wife died during childbirth. Sonora was a member of Old Centenary Presbyterian Church (now Knox Presbyterian Church), where she first proposed the idea of a day to honor fathers. After hearing a sermon about Mother's Day in 1909 at Central Methodist Episcopal Church, she told her pastor that fathers should have a similar day. Several local clergymen accepted the idea, and on June 19, 1910, a celebration was held at the YMCA in Spokane, Washington. That idea of a Father's Day observance stuck and grew to nearly world-wide recognition.

Like many other holidays, however, this observance has lost some of its real meaning over the years. It has become commercialized. Online and offline we are bombarded by special offers to buy dad a smart phone, a home theater system, gift cards, golf clubs or cloth-ing. Gifts are good, but what would it be like if those who are able would **also** spend time with their father? It's free. Take a walk. Talk. Reminisce. Tell him you love him. Give him a hug. As years go by both of you will fondly remember the great times you spent together on father's days, long after the gift is forgotten.

God is a Father too. Remember Him?

BY HOOK OR BY CROOK

Where did that expression ever come from? I've used the saying myself but until recently didn't know how it originated.

In feudal days of the Medieval Age, the lord of the manor did not allow his peasant workers to cut down trees for firewood. Instead they could use only the limbs they could cut down with a pruning hook or pull down with a shepherd's crook. Along with pieces lying on the ground, they had to be content with what they could obtain by hook or by crook.

We are indeed very fortunate not to be restricted to those conditions. In fact, most of us would have a hard time remembering when we last used wood to heat our homes. In addition many of us have freedoms, food, funds and family to enjoy that are not constrained by a mean boss. Most of us are surrounded by the benefits of nature, the stocked shelves of stores and the kindness of friends. Few of us are limited to what we can pull in *by hook or by crook*. We indeed have much to be thankful for. Thanksgiving Day is coming.

LANGUAGES OF LOVE

Valentine's Day is meant to be a time to express love. Cards and gifts can help to do that, but, if we try to salve our conscience by sending a card or gift in hopes of making up for shortcomings, they won't fill the gap. In his book, *The Five Love Languages,* (sold 7 million copies in English alone plus many in 49 other languages), Dr. Gary Chapman claimed that most people relate best to one or two of the following five options: meaningful gifts, words of affirmation, quality time, endearing physical touches or genuine acts of service. Whether it is family, spouse, neighbor, friend or work associate, one or more of these will be particularly valued by the recipient and help to cement a positive relationship. A valentine card may be very appropriate for some situations but for others it just wouldn't be enough. Nor does the fact that Valentine's Day may already be passed mean we've lost the opportunity, the year ahead will present many chances.

It is not easy to determine which one is right for you, but it is worth the effort. It is even more difficult to consistently practice it, (I know that from experience) but think of what the opposite does to people.

Shall we call them the five languages of hate or resentment? They would be obsessive greed, negative criticism, cold withdrawal, cruel violence and outright selfishness. It's our move!

MOTHERING

Mother's Day is filled with sharply contrasting situations.

Some mothers are excitedly expecting a first child, others are struggling with the empty nest syndrome.

Some are rejoicing at family gatherings on this day while others are grieving over loss, infertility, miscarriage or a broken relationship with a child.

Some remember mother as a best friend, a few may even think of her as an abusive fiend.

Some are weary from the strain of boisterous littles ones around all day, while others bask in the love of compliant children.

Whatever the circumstances are for you, mother, be encouraged. You are very precious!

MOTHERS AND MAGNETS

The list of things that mothers do for children is very, very long. On Mother's Day we do well to acknowledge the huge debt we owe to all those patient, caring and self-sacrificing mothers who kept doing the right thing in spite of often getting no thanks in return. Hopefully you will be assured today that you are appreciated. But it isn't always the huge heroic deeds that stand out in a child's mind, as is illustrated by the following incident.

A teacher's lesson for her Grade Two class was all about magnets. She demonstrated how it could pick up pins, nails and other small iron items. Then she explained how a bigger magnet can pick up bigger items. Finally she showed them pictures of a crane that could even use a huge magnet to pick up cars in a salvage yard. At the end of the lesson period she wanted to be sure that they remembered the word magnet. So she asked the class one question. If my name starts with M and I can pick up a lot of things that are lying around what am I?

One boy piped up and said, "You are a mother".

A MOTHER'S SACRIFICE

Scene 1: Three girls are walking down the street. They spot a disfigured woman. Scars cover her face and arms. The girls engage in ridiculing remarks. "Look at that ugly woman." "She ought to stay off the street." "I wouldn't want to be seen dead with her!" Laughter and derision mark their attitudes, although one girl seems uncomfortable. Their comments are loud enough to be heard by the woman. She glances at them with obvious pain and hurt, but says nothing.

Scene 2: Same girls, same location; different response from one of them. After two of the girls indulge in derogatory remarks the third one speaks up with passion. "That is my mother! When I was only four she risked her life to save me from a burning building. In the course of protecting me her face and hands were severely burned. I owe my life to her and I love her. Every scar on her body is precious to me!" The other two girls were embarrassed and humiliated. A major decision faced them. They had to choose between deep, humbling apologies and requests for forgiveness, or else walk away and scoff at the girl who spoke up.

Few mothers have had to endure the rebuff of scene one, but many mothers have given significant, self-sacrificing acts of love that have not been appreciated. A big Mother's Day 'thank you' for the sacrifices they have made for us.

NO TURNING BACK

At this time of year Remembrance Day causes us to reflect on the bravery of soldiers as well as the ugliness of war. In Scripture, life itself is often likened to a battle. The following accounts apply to those times when life feels like a war going on inside of us.

In the momentous battle of Waterloo Napolean's army captured a highland piper. Intrigued by the determined attitude of the prisoner Napolean asked him to play a tune for them. He did. Play a march. He did. Play a retreat. "Nay, nay," replied the highlander, "that I cannot do. I never learned to play one."

General Washington and his army crossed a bridge at Brandywine Creek during the Revolutionary War. "General, shall we burn the bridge or leave it there?" asked one of his men. "We might need it to make good a retreat." "Burn it", was the reply, "we'll have victory or death. There will be no retreat."

While there is wisdom in some forms of retreat during ordinary life we also know that when it comes to the goal of our Christian life, the Lord will give us strength to keep moving forward.

Stay with it, it's sunny up ahead.

POWER

On July 1, 1867 the governing authorities implemented a powerful decision that formed the dominion of Canada. This has impacted all of us in significant ways. We are blessed to be living in Canada. Every time I've been to another country I've looked forward to coming back to Canada. It is truly one of the best on the planet! That privilege also calls for us to respond with gratefulness, integrity and wisdom! Unfortunately some politicians in some countries want to use benefits and wield power for personal aggrandizement or unwarranted control over others.

Thankfully there is a different kind of power at work in the world as well. It is the power of the gospel that can transform people for better purposes than selfish ambition.

"I am not ashamed of the gospel, because it is the power of God for the salvation of everyone who believes..." Romans 1:16

It is not a power that generates political impositions from the outside, but one that transforms people on the inside. The word 'gospel' means good news. The good news is that God loves each one of us enough to cause Jesus to shed His life blood for us as payment for our wrongs. In addition He then offers us guidance and ability to also change the way we live. Now that is a huge gift!

That kind of power will put us on the sunny side.

HONORING THEIR MEMORY

It was a warm sunny day. The pleasant walk took these hikers past a veteran's cemetery in Grand Rapids, Michigan. A large monument in that cemetery contained the engraved names of 225 men who had given their lives for their country. The future had lain before them as a life they hoped to enjoy but it was cut short. Their sacrifice was huge. It deserved thanks and respect.

However, stretched out on top of the monument was a young fellow in a sleeveless shirt, sunglasses and shorts catching the rays. On his stomach was a boom box belting out the latest hits. Undoubtedly he was enjoying the benefits of the day.

Think of it! Below him were the names of some who had purchased his freedom to enjoy the day (whether U.S. or Canada), even though they themselves would never have the opportunity to do so. Without their sacrifice life could have been very different for him but he seemed to be unaware and unthankful. Not a thought seems to have been given to what it cost to preserve his freedom. It may be that he intended no harm but it also is probably not too severe to call that action disrespectful.

Will this day be just a holiday for me?

REMEMBRANCE

How does a person go about remembering something he/she has not experienced? How can anyone identify with an event he/she was not part of? It requires ingenuity and reflection.

I was born just before WW2 began. At our place in Northern Ontario the effects of that war were remote. I have only one memory associated with WW2. I remember drawing airplane fights in the sky and pretending to shoot them down. It seemed exciting, but I had no concept of the ugliness of that battle. With siblings I probably transferred that to imaginary gun battles using wooden sticks, totally unaware of the implications.

Shortly after the war was over our family moved to the Fraser Valley in B.C. Over the years economic growth, technological advantages, increased opportunities to pursue fulfilling careers and many other benefits of life in a peaceful society made thinking of sacrifices in war a remote consideration. You don't feel the pain if you haven't been hurt. The memories aren't there.

But that is a problem. I benefitted because others sacrificed. Therefore I had better remember.

WAR AND PEACE

Remembering war, its heroes and its consequences goes back a long, long way. Hoping and wishing that there would be peace goes back even farther.

Have you ever repeatedly asked God for a solution to this? Have you ever chafed at the sight of violence against innocent people day after day and complained that nothing is being done about it? Not even God seems to get involved. Have you ever despaired over how long this is going to go on before something is done?

Over 2500 years ago the prophet Habakkuk asked the same questions. You can read about it in the Old Testament book by his name. In chapter two he makes it clear that **prestige** (vs. 4 – ego), **pleasure** (vs. 5 – selfish motives), **possessions** (v. 5 – greed) and **power** (vs. 5 – zeal to conquer) were among the motives that drove the Babylonians to conquer others. Has anything changed? Are not these same four pursuits society's downfall today **<u>if they are the priority</u>**? There is a place in life for all four but if one or more of them become the most important pursuit in life instead of love for God and love for people we are headed for deep trouble.

So what is God's answer to why He doesn't intervene? Some day He will mete out justice but right now He is patiently waiting for people to respond to His love. The last chapter is yet to be written.

SAVING PRIVATE RYAN

A fitting perspective for Remembrance Day.

During the disastrous WW2 Normandy Invasion at Omaha Beach, three Ryan brothers were killed. A fourth, James, survived and continued to fight against enemy lines. Army officials in Washington instructed Captain Miller to find James Ryan and send him home to his mother lest she lose a fourth son. Capt. Miller and seven others set out to find him. In the course of the search two of the seven men were killed. Upon reaching James Ryan at the Meredith River defending an important bridge, James listened to the request, was deeply saddened, but wanted to stay in the battle. The captain and the five remaining men chose to stay with him and join the battle. During that battle the captain and four more men died. The captain's last words to Private Ryan were, *"James, earn this. Earn it!"*

What a heavy load that must have been for Ryan to carry after he managed to survive and get back to America. For about 50 years he struggled with the challenge of earning the price six men paid with their lives for his survival. The elderly private Ryan visited the captain's gravesite under deep conviction and pleaded with his wife to say that he had lived a good life and earned the right to live. His wife said he had. Upon this confirmation James Ryan saluted the captain's gravesite and left somewhat relieved.

That is a powerful story. On Remembrance weekend it vividly sets out the awful cost of war. Ryan's desire to merit his survival was very commendable. But we also have had Someone die for us. According to Scripture the *"wages of sin is death" Romans 6:23,* but thankfully *"the gift of God is eternal life".* This was made possible because Jesus died for us. The price has already been paid. We do not and cannot earn it. What we can do is admit that we need it and accept it as a gift. Then we need to live for the One who gave us such an incredible gift.

Overwhelmed to be on the sunny side by grace.

WHAT IS LOVE?

Valentine's Day is associated with expressions of love. I suspect that many people have an incomplete picture of what love is. There are at least three major categories or levels of love. Apparently the Greek language of the New Testament used three different words to identify these three kinds which the English language lumps together under one word, love.

"Agape" love is a **decision**, an act of the will. It does not ask for merit in the person being loved. It simply is based on a decision to do what is best for the other person whether they deserve it or not. This is the kind of love God has for people. It is also possible for people to have this attitude toward others, most notably found in a parent's love for the baby.

"Philos" love is sometimes a **duty**, an action based on obligation, but more often based on kinship. It is most easily noticed in a family setting where you stick up for your brother, sister, cousin, child, or parent because you are related. It is kindness extended to someone who belongs to your group even if they sometimes irritate you. It is also known as brotherly love or the love for a friend.

"Eros" love is motivated by **desire** and is chiefly centered on sexual attraction. It easily degenerates into a self-centered action. In its most ugly form we see abuse and rape. In its most positive form it expresses a beautiful picture of sincere love and ensures the propagation of the species.

There is a place for all three, an important place. Unfortunately, the last definition is the most prevalent one and the first is least often achieved by us. We have reversed the order of importance. May your Valentine's Day, and mine, at least show some true love.

TO MOTHER

Philadelphia's philanthropist, John Wanamaker, wrote this about his mother when he was 80 years old.

My first love was my mother, and my first home was upon her breast. My first bed was her bosom. Leaning my little arms upon her knees, I learned my first prayers. A bright lamp she lighted in my soul, that never dies down nor goes out, though the winds and waves of fourscore years haves swept over me. Sitting in my mother's own armchair which she loved - because her first born son gave it to her forty years ago — I am writing this in the evening twilight. With the darkness falling, I seem to lose myself in the flood of sweet memories, and to feel that the arms of the chair have loosed themselves to become my very own mother's arms around me again, drawing me to her bosom, the happiest place on earth, just as she used to do in the days and nights long gone by. I feel that touch of her little hand on my brow, and in memory I hear her voice as she smooths my hair and calls me her boy, her very own boy!

That is a great tribute!

THEME 10

Influence and Achievement

Most people hope for some meaning in life related to their influence and achievement.

"You are the salt of the earth." Matthew 5:13

ALEXANDER GRAHAM BELL

Alexander Bell wanted to find a way to more effectively communicate with his hearing impaired mother. His father's work in speech pathology aided this lifelong interest. At the University of London, Herman von Helmholtz's work with electrical tuning forks intrigued him. Lacking sufficient knowledge of German, Alexander misinterpreted Helmholtz's theory and thought it meant that sound could be transmitted over a wire. Later on Bell admitted, *"If I had been able to read German, I might never have begun my experiments in electricity."* But those experiments led to the invention of the telephone. At that time it would have been considered a wild speculation, bordering on crazy, to say that your voice could travel to Europe (or even to the next town) on a wire. He invented other devices too but this is his most prominent and best known achievement. It was a great achievement for which we are profoundly grateful.

We rightfully honor him for this achievement but let's not forget the One who built this potential into wires and electricity. God created the potential, Bell discovered it. People are still discovering marvelous potentials in nature. They are amazing achievements, but this kind of science depends on the predictability of the laws of nature put there by the Creator.

CLOCKS

Historians have credited the Chinese Emperor, Hwangti, with developing the first clock about 4000 years ago. He apparently did it by placing a small boat into a large basin. The boat had a small hole in it. Presumably a mark at the waterline at the start and another one after a full day had passed (or when it sank) would allow him to calibrate a predetermined number of segments. I don't know if they chose 24 for a full day. An advance on this plan had water dripping onto geared paddle wheels, thus moving hands over twelve evenly spaced markers.

Later notched candles and hourglasses solved freezing weather problems for water clocks. After that, blacksmiths are credited with building enormous geared devices for 24 hour clocks. The king of France had one built in 1360 that lasted for nearly 500 years with few repairs. Now an atomic clock using microscopic ammonia molecules has been invented that claims to be able to divide a second into 24 billion parts! (Who's counting?) Regardless of how it is measured, time is precious.

That's why Paul's letter to the Ephesians admonished them to "*redeem the time*". That can only be done by using it profitably. We each have a limited amount and none of us can be sure when that time runs out. What we do know is that now is the time to make sure that our relationship with the Creator is in good shape. It surely is comforting to know that if we acknowledge our accountability, admit our sinfulness and ask His forgiveness He freely gives it.

COOL AS A CUCUMBER

Where did that expression come from? It is apparently based on facts that can be easily tested when you have a cucumber plant in your garden. Even in hot weather the core of the cucumber remains about ten degrees cooler than the outer 'skin'. If a cucumber is severed from the plant that does not happen anymore. The reason is that the plant keeps circulating plant juices that keep the core cooler or else it will spoil. That design feature is the result of a purposeful, creative plan. It also contains a life lesson for us.

Sometimes we get hot and bothered about what is happening to us. You might say the heat is getting to us. But if we are connected to the One who created us and maintain trust in His cooling advice for us, we can get through those troubling times as cool as a cucumber.

So, let's keep cool.

DRONES

Drones have become big business. Many are fascinated with what they can do, whether for recreation or for business. Word has it that you can buy a drone that automatically will head for home and the charger if the battery gets too low.

Ever felt that your own body's battery is low? You've just had too much stress, too many responsibilities or too many frustrations. You just wish you could go somewhere to recharge. You are so drained. Maybe we can learn from this drone? We just have to head for home. But where is home when you are emotionally and spiritually drained? It's time to recall the words of Jesus who said, *"Come to Me all you who labor and are heavy laden, I will give you rest."* Matthew 11:28 That is a huge promise. Can He really do that? Could it be that we are trying to do on our own strength what we were never meant to undertake? Could it be that He can provide the wisdom we need to sort things out, drop some commitments or find a better way to deal with them?

When your battery is low, turn around and come home for recharging.

FRANKLIN EXPEDITION INTO THE NORTHWEST PASSAGE

On May 5, 1845, John Franklin received his official instructions to map the remaining 500 kilometers of the Arctic coastline to hopefully achieve a Northwest Passage. A crew of 129 left in two sailships with a three year's supply of food, a 1200 volume library, fine china, crystal goblets and sterling silverware but only a 12 day supply of coal for the auxiliary steam engines. The ships became trapped in vast frozen plains of ice. After several months, Lord Franklin died. It is likely that improperly lead-sealed cans of food became poisoned.

The men decided to trek to safety in small groups but none of them survived.

After not hearing from them for two years Lady Franklin appealed for a search party but the Admiralty delayed because they had a three year supply of food. Later, many search parties went out to find them due to the lure of financial rewards but more people died in the search than in the expedition. A particularly heart-breaking story tells of finding the remains of two officers who had pulled a large sled for 65 miles. The sled was filled with silverware. When the situation became desperate the men realized they had with them many things that were of no help and the essentials they had counted on were fatally contaminated.

In the year ahead of us, will we be found to burden ourselves with treasures that are of no help and resources that fail to meet our needs? When life is over and we stand before God we will realize that if we have invested our lives in temporal treasures or chosen to depend on our own merits to see us through, those ideas will fail. *"All have sinned and fall short..." Romans 3:23.* Having paid the price, Jesus offers lasting and fulfilling provision for those who in this life have admitted their need of a Savior who forgives sin and trusted Him with the problem. That offer of grace can be yours too. It is the real deal!

GPS FOR THE SOUL

Many of us travel with GPS, a Global Positioning System tracking device, in the car. Using satellite technology it can tell you where you are and how to get to your destination. I thought of how we need GPS for our soul, our life, not just for the car. Here's a comparison.

The car gets information via satellite mapping, but the soul gets advice from God by way of the Bible and fellow believers.

GPS tells the car driver where he/she is at geographically, but the Bible tells you where you are at spiritually.

GPS directions are usually appreciated but God's advice is seldom appreciated.

GPS will redirect the route if you get off the path. The Bible will redirect you if you stray.

The voice on GPS offers neither compassion nor criticism if you refuse to take its advice. The 'voice' of God will encourage what's right and send warnings about wrong choices.

GPS has the one goal of reaching your choice of destination. God has the one goal of having you reach His best plan for your destination.

GPS directs you where **you want** to go. The Bible directs you where **you should** go.

Would you like to have GPS for your soul? Here is good news. God is waiting for you to log in.

"Trust in the Lord with all your heart and lean not on your own understanding; in all your ways acknowledge Him and He will make your paths straight." Proverbs 3:5-6

I DON'T UNDERSTAND

As I am typing this the computer is translating my keyboard strokes into words on the screen. I don't know how it does that but I count on it anyway. If I instruct the computer to insert a colored graphic it does that too. How? – I don't know. If I punch the right letters and numbers on the keyboard it will connect me to someone on the other side of the world, do mathematical calculations, bring up information on a topic of my choosing, receive emails from a friend, and who knows what else. I depend on it to do all that even though I don't comprehend just how it will all come together.

There's a similarity between this and the prophet statement that *"… my thoughts are not your thoughts, neither are your ways my ways." Isaiah 55:8*

Even though I have unanswered questions in my mind about why things are the way they are I conclude by deciding as follows. I will let my life be guided by answers I can't question rather than questions I can't answer.

There's peace on the sunny side.

INFLUENCE

Who has been the most influential person of the last 2000 years? If we applied the criteria that follow, who would likely come out on top?

- multitudes of followers for all of the last 2000 years
- more than many thousands of books written about him/her
- people willing to suffer and even die for that person, though they likely never met him/her in person
- has radically changed millions of people's lives, including rescue from dissolute and criminal lives
- well known around the world
- has left a legacy on how to live life with meaning
- and more…

Some statisticians correctly tell us that it would be Jesus Christ. Yet He did this without pursuing celebrity status. In fact He was hated, persecuted and eventually crucified at age 33. He gained worldwide renown without ever having left the land of Israel since infancy. He wrote no books himself, owned very few possessions, associated freely with outcasts as well as royalty without being swayed by either, and taught truth boldly. He worked as a carpenter in a remote village until age 30, leaving only about 3 ½ years to make His mark on history. There is a season of the year that is supposed to be devoted to recognizing His birth, yet many in our country would prefer to leave Him out of it completely.

I am grateful for His influence on me and want to make Him central.

MARIE CURIE

Born Maria Sklodowska in Poland (1867) to a pianist mother and a university professor father, she showed an early interest in getting an education. She won awards for academic achievement and had hopes of pursuing advanced education but an unwise investment by the father dashed those hopes. She agreed to work as a governess in order to finance her sister Bronia's education, who then would do the reverse for Maria. Both kept their promises but serious hurdles stood in the way of accomplishing Maria's dreams.

A sad love affair plagued her time as a governess.

At Sorbonne, Paris, she lived in cramped student quarters surviving mainly on bread, butter and tea.

She married Pierre Curie in 1895 and both of them committed themselves to the study of radium and polonium, elements they had isolated in very poor laboratory conditions. She adopted the French version of her name, Marie.

In addition to scientific research, they spent hours teaching in order to support themselves and their two daughters.

In spite of those hurdles they, together with Antoine Henri Bequerel, won the Nobel Prize for Physics in 1904.

Intense work leading to the discovery of radioactivity was tragically marred when Pierre was killed in a traffic accident.

Soon after this devastating event Marie recovered and was asked to take Pierre's teaching position at Sorbonne, becoming the first woman teacher there.

Another achievement rewarded her dedication as she won a second Nobel Prize in 1911. This time for Chemistry. This was followed by finding therapeutic use for radium in the medical field, but she didn't realize the danger of frequent exposure to radioactivity. Eventually it was a major contributor to her death.

It's a lesson in prevailing in spite of adversity!

PIONEER TRAVEL

I was feeling sorry for travelers in pioneer or ancient days. Settlers of the west in their bone-jarring wagons, Mary on her way to Bethlehem on a donkey late in her pregnancy, Moses and a horde of Israelites on foot in the Sinai wilderness for 40 years, and Abram gathering all he had on his camels to re-settle in a country he'd never seen. They must all have had tough and exhausting trips. They likely were minus almost all the comforts of life and knew little about what was happening around them.

I felt sorry for them as I was sitting in the cushioned comfort of an air-conditioned car. A push of the button would put me in touch with the latest news, a symphony orchestra or a sporting event. My GPS would keep me on target if the route was unfamiliar. Another button would use Bluetooth technology for hands-free cell phone use with almost anyone I chose to talk to. At intervals I could pull into a drive-through for coffee and donuts. If there were grandchildren in the back seat one could be sure that an MP3, an iPod, iPad, or whatever newfangled gadget had come out, would keep them entertained. They'd be tweeting and texting with friends, or in touch with World Wide Websites on the internet. What a contrast to the pioneers!! Those poor travelers.

Then I took a closer look at the experiences of Abram, Moses and Mary. They had been in touch with Someone that far exceeded all the abilities of Facebook, Twitter, Instagram or the web. They had heard from God directly. Their lives were not without pain and struggles but vision, mission and fulfillment in life were theirs. No one is going to talk about my trip in the car even a week from now. But we talk about Abram, Moses and Mary after thousands of years. Who is the one to feel sorry about? We get caught up in the tangle of all our inventions, obsessed with the toys of our day and miss out on the meaning of life **if** on those electronic devices we hear from everyone and everywhere except God. The meaning of life is found in relationships. The Gospel of Mark in 12:30-31 makes it clear that our relationships with God and then with others are #1 and #2 in importance. Who is the one losing out?

THERMOMETERS AND THERMOSTATS

Am I like a thermometer or more like a thermostat? A thermometer simply reflects the temperature of its surroundings. It does not, and cannot, influence changes. However, a thermostat can bring about changes in the temperature of its surroundings. It is a change agent, it carries the power to influence its environment.

If I am like a thermometer I simply reflect conditions around me. If I'm in a conflict environment I become angry and combative just like the rest. If I'm in a happy situation, I join in with the laughter. If people are negative or sad I become negative or sad too.

But if I am like a thermostat I will make a difference. I will seek to decrease the heated temperature of a conflict. I will instill some joy into a negative situation. I may be able to help lift someone out of the slough of despondency. I can become a change agent to at least some degree.

So, am I, are you, like a thermometer or more like a thermostat?

Let's make a difference, in the right way, when things need to be changed.

WINDSHIELD WIPERS

There may well have been a time when some of us had to drive along a highway that was a mass of dirty slush. Every approaching car threw up a flood of dirty slush the completely obscured our vision. Danger was averted by the windshield wiper. But a wiper alone would have only smeared the mud, creating an opaque film. A press of the button caused the windshield washer to squirt clean water onto the windshield and cleared it up. When that water supply ran out it became important to replenish it.

Come to think of it, we are equipped with windshield wipers and washers that existed long before cars had them. Our eyelids work 24/7 to clean our 'windshield'. Not only that, our eyes are provided with tiny tear ducts that make these wipers able to keep it clear and clean. God thought of everything when He created us.

The Bible compares itself to water that cleanses. We can keep that supply from being empty by regularly reading and meditating on God's Word.

"How can a young person stay on the path of purity? By living according to your word." Psalm 119:9

THEME 11

Kindness

It is claimed that kindness is one of the most important ingredients for a good relationship.

"Love is patient, love is kind." 1 Corinthians 13:4

THANKFUL FOR ACTS OF KINDNESS

How do we cope with another senseless massacre on a weekend when we are supposed to be thankful? One thing we can do is remember that there still is kindness in action in many places. This was written by a Metro Denver Hospice Physician some years ago. Its authenticity has been challenged, but if fictional, it still sends a good message.

I was driving home from a meeting this evening about five, stuck in traffic on Colorado Blvd., and the car started to choke and splutter and die. I barely managed to coast into a gas station, glad only that I would not be blocking traffic and would have a somewhat warm spot to wait for the tow truck. Before I could make the call, I saw a woman walking out of the quickie mart building, and it looked like she slipped on some ice and fell into a gas pump, so I got out to see if she was okay. When I got there, it looked more like she had been overcome by sobs than that she had fallen. She was a young woman who looked really haggard with dark circles under her eyes. She dropped something as I helped her up, and I picked it up to give it to her. It was a nickel.

At that moment, everything came into focus for me: the crying woman, the ancient Suburban crammed full of stuff with three kids in the back (one in a car seat), and the gas pump reading $4.95. I asked her if she was okay and if she needed help, and she just kept saying, "I don't want my kids to see me crying!" So we stood on the other side of the pump from her car. She said she was driving to California and that things were very hard for her right now. So I asked, "And you were praying?" That made her back away from me a little, but I assured her I was not a crazy person and said, "He heard you, and He sent me."

I took out my card and swiped it through the card reader on the pump so she could fill up her car completely, and while it was fueling, walked to the next door McDonald's and bought two big bags of food, some gift certificates for more, and a big cup of coffee. She gave the food to the kids in the car, who attacked it like wolves, and we stood by the pump eating fries and talking a little.

She told me her name, and that she lived in Kansas City. Her boyfriend left two months ago and she had not been able to make ends meet. She knew she wouldn't have money to pay rent Jan. 1, and finally, in desperation, had called her parents, with whom she had not spoken in about five years. They lived in California and said she could come live with them and try to get on her feet there. So she packed up everything she owned in the car. I gave her my gloves, a little hug and said a quick prayer with her for safety on the road. As I was walking over to my car, she said, "So, are you like an angel or something?" This definitely made me cry. I said, "Sweetie, at this time of year angels are really busy, so sometimes God uses regular people." It was so incredible to be a part of someone else's miracle. And of course, you guessed it, when I got into my car it started right away and got me home with no problem. I'll put it into the shop tomorrow to check, but I suspect the mechanic won't find anything wrong.

SACRIFICIAL KINDNESS

A party of explorers stumbled into hard times as they neared the South Pole. Heavy snowfall had slowed down the expedition and they were now at risk of not making it back to their base camp. Their food supply had dwindled to the point where each of them were left with only a few biscuits in their knapsacks. That night the leader stirred uneasily in his sleep. Half-awake he saw one member stretching out his hand toward the youngest explorer's knapsack. Was he so desperate that he would steal from a comrade? Had he sunk so low as to become a thief? This would be a crime almost as serious as murder. Then he noticed that the man wasn't taking a biscuit out of the knapsack, but half of one into the younger man's knapsack. This younger man had shown signs of failing strength and this was an act of kindness, however small. The leader felt a warm glow within in spite of the bitter cold.

Small acts of kindness can bring in big sunshine.

GOOD DEEDS

He almost didn't see the old lady, stranded on the side of the road. But even in the dim light of day, he could see she needed help. So he pulled up in front of her Mercedes and got out. His Pontiac was still sputtering when he approached her.

Even with the smile on his face, she was worried. No one had stopped to help for the last hour or so. Was he going to hurt her? He didn't look safe, he looked poor and hungry. He could see that she was frightened, standing out there in the cold. He knew how she felt. It was that chill which only fear can put in you. He said, "I'm here to help you, ma'am. Why don't you wait in the car where it's warm? By the way, my name is Bryan."

Well, all she had was a flat tire, but for an old lady, that was bad enough. Bryan crawled under the car looking for a place to put the jack, skinning his knuckles a time or two. Soon he was able to change the tire. But he had to get dirty and his hands hurt. As he was tightening up the lug nuts, she rolled down the window and began to talk to him. She told him that she was from St. Louis and was only just passing through. She couldn't thank him enough for coming to her aid. Bryan just smiled as he closed her trunk. She asked him how much she owed him. Any amount would have been all right with her. She already imagined all the awful things that could have happened had he not stopped.

Bryan never thought twice about being paid. This was not a job to him. This was helping someone in need, and God knows there were plenty who had given him a hand in the past. He had lived his whole life that way, and it never occurred to him to act any other way.

He told her that if she really wanted to pay him back, the next time she saw someone who needed help, she could give that person the assistance they needed, and Bryan added, "And think of me." He waited until she started her car and drove off. It had been a cold and depressing day, but he felt good as he headed for home and disappeared into the twilight.

A few miles down the road the lady saw a small cafe. She went in to grab a bite to eat, and take the chill off before she made the last leg of her trip home. It was a dingy looking restaurant. Outside were two old gas pumps. The whole scene was unfamiliar to her. The cash register was like the telephone of an out-of-work actor, it didn't ring much. The waitress came over and brought a clean towel to wipe her wet hair.

She had a sweet smile, one that even being on her feet for the whole day couldn't erase. The lady noticed the waitress was nearly eight months pregnant, but she never let the strain and aches change her attitude. The old lady wondered how someone who had so little could be so giving to a stranger. Then she remembered Bryan.

After the lady finished her meal, and the waitress went to get change for her hundred dollar bill, the lady slipped right out the door. She was gone by the time the waitress came back. The waitress wondered where the lady could be. Then she noticed something written on the napkin under which were four $100 bills. There were tears in her eyes when she read what the lady wrote: "You don't owe me anything. I have been there too. Somebody once helped me out, the way I'm helping you. If you really want to pay me back, here is what you do: Do not let this chain of love end with you."

Well, there were tables to clear, sugar bowls to fill, and people to serve, but the waitress made it through another day. That night when she got home from work and climbed into bed, she was thinking about the money and what the lady had written. How could the lady have known how much she and her husband needed it? With the baby due next month, it was going to be hard. She knew how worried her husband was, and as he lay sleeping next to her, she gave him a soft kiss and whispered soft and low, "Everything's gonna be all right. I love you, Bryan."

Author Unknown

I cannot prove that this really happened, though it likely did, but if it is just a story it's a really good one.

CHRISTIAN KINDNESS

A Texas pastor, Rev. Baumgartel, tells the story of how he saw his father show unusual kindness to a neighbor when this pastor was still a child. He had paid the neighbor to deliver a ton of coal to his coal bin. The coal was delivered while the family was away for the day. The son checked the coal bin and indignantly reported to the father that the neighbor had only delivered half a ton! The father instructed the son to say nothing about the matter.

Several weeks later the neighbor's house caught on fire. The family lost everything. The pastor's father graciously housed the whole family until arrangements could be made. The son struggled with resentment when he was assigned to the barn loft so that the neighbor could use his bedroom. This wasn't fair!

Early one morning he overheard a conversation between his father and the neighbor as they were working in the barn below him. "You have been kind to me," the neighbor remarked, "even though I cheated you out of half a ton of coal a while ago." Amid broken hearted sobs he pled, "I want you to forgive me." Forgiveness was granted. At that point the neighbor decided he needed the faith and love that the pastor showed.

Love in action is a powerful way to move things on to the sunny side.

MISDIRECTED COMPLIMENTS

A group of friends had gathered in a home for an evening of fun, food and fellowship. One person in the group was a photographer who took great pains to produce good work. As the pictures were being admired while they were passed around, the hostess remarked, "These are really good. You must have a very expensive camera."

The photographer did not say anything in response. After the meal was over, the hostess was being rightfully complimented for the delicious feast she had prepared. The photographer couldn't resist the comment, "That meal was really great. You must have an expensive set of pots and pans."

Not everything we say comes across to the recipient with the meaning we had intended. Psalm 19:14 *"May the words of my mouth and the meditations of my heart be pleasing in your sight, LORD."*

It's hard to always think before we speak.

OIL

Oil has qualities that are instructive for our lives.

- It reduces friction. When conflicts arise, and there is more heat than light in the discussion, someone in the group is wise to spread a bit of the oil of good cheer on the rough spots.
- Oil doesn't mix with water. There are things in life that we just can't allow to integrate with ours.
- Some oils have healing qualities. The object lesson is self-evident.
- Some oils spread a sweet fragrance. It's great to have some of that around in life.
- Certain oils can be used as a fuel for an engine. It will provide the energy to get work done. That quality in a person is valuable.

Spread a little of the oil of gladness.

A PERILOUS TREK

With no compass and only a roughly sketched map of the northern Ontario wilderness, Doug Rickard, age nineteen, embarked on a trek to the nearest major road north of Kapuskasing. The twists and turns he'd have to take would nearly double the direct distance of 75 km. Neither the -20 degree weather nor the lack of a trail through the deep snow was going to stop him. His mother was suffering from a stroke and he was going for help. The long walk would take a week or more.

The five Cree in this family were trappers, scheduled to be picked up after two more weeks. Then the stroke hit. The mother did not want the father, Fred, to go so the son offered to get help. Wearing his backpack filled with a knife, rope, moccasins, winter boots, heavy socks, flour, tea, kettle, sugar, lard, matches, small ax, blanket, sleeping bag and an extra set of clothes, he set out on his snow shoes.

Each night he had to find a sheltered grove, make a bed of pine boughs, build a small lean-to shelter, gather wood for a fire, try to dry out soaked clothes and then get some sleep. Each morning he arose to a very cold campsite. Then he faced the insecurity of a crude map, detours around gullies or thick underbrush, energy draining away and the worries about becoming lost. But then a clearing opened up. He had found a road. It must lead to the Smoky Falls road that he needed, but three more days of walking yielded no sight of any civilization. He came upon a small Ontario Hydro generating station but there was nobody there. An hour and a half later a truck came around the bend. Randy Orr and Gerald Bernard, hydro workers, spotted Doug and picked him up. They couldn't believe he had been walking through the wilderness for seven days. An hour later a Spruce Falls helicopter picked Doug up. It took only 30 minutes to reach the Rickard cottage. It was an unbelievably excited reunion. The mother had not only survived but regained a fair bit of her health. She was flown to Moose Factory General Hospital. Doug was awarded the OPP bravery award for his incredible achievement of endurance and courage. Well deserved.

Based on the November, 1984 Readers' Digest article.

This story had special meaning for me, having lived the first nine years of my life about 50 km out of Kapuskasing.

SCHLUMBERGERA

In 2018 I brought home a Schlumbergera Christmas Cactus for my wife. It was a small plant, probably not yet mature. It produced a lot of flower buds but they all withered and fell off. We wondered if we should just toss the plant out as a failure. But we didn't. In November of 2019 it produced another prolific set of buds. This time they bloomed in profusion. The flowers were not ordinary, they were delicate and very attractive. It was a marvelous display of beauty. Here we sat in wonder as we remembered that we had almost thrown it away. Perhaps we need a more patient approach and it deserves a prettier name.

Do we treat people that way too? Are we ready to throw some of them away because they don't seem to produce anything worthwhile? It is thought provoking to realize how often Jesus hung out with the downcast, the rejects, the despised and the broken. He helped, healed and comforted them. Then he declared that whatever you do for "the least of these", you have done for Me. (Matthew 25:45) Remember that they too were made in the image of God, which means to have a mind, a will and emotions.

There are many people around us who need encouragement.

ACTS OF KINDNESS

I stopped at the Post Office on the way home from a pre-Christmas dinner with a group of friends. Helen was anxious to get home rather than wait in the car and get cold. I said that if the line-up was too long I'd go back to the Post Office later. The lineup was short. All I needed was to find out if the bulky envelope needed more postage. It needed another 35 cents. I had no change in my pocket. Not only that – my wallet wasn't with me either. I told the clerk I'd have to go to the car to look for my wallet and I'd be right back. Greg Casorso was also in the Post Office and offered to spare me the effort by providing the 35 cents. I gratefully accepted the help and rushed back to the car. At home I started to look for my wallet in the car. Couldn't find it. Eventually I remembered that I had put it into the side pocket of my laptop carrying bag. Had Greg not offered me the

35 cents I would have been engaged in a very frustrating search and Helen in an even more anxious dilemma?

Thank you, Lord, and Greg, for a small act of kindness that prevented a big embarrassment. We may often think that a little act of caring for someone else is no big deal, but it is.

SMALL THINGS

Little things can cause big trouble, but they can also solve big problems. Years ago, the '74 LTD Ford we owned refused to start. I'm not a mechanic but I wanted to check things out in case it was just some little thing. There was enough gas, the battery was doing fine and the starter was functioning. What could it be? Being an older car the distributer cap and rotor were still part of the ignition system. After removing the cap I discovered that one small plastic part was broken. For 90 cents (this was years ago) I was able to buy a replacement part and the car was back on the road.

It isn't always the big things people do that bring joy or show care. Sometimes there are little deeds of kindness and a few words of understanding that can make the difference. I recall a children's song:

> *Little drops of water, little grains of sand,*
> *Make a mighty ocean and a pleasant land.*
> *Little deeds of kindness, little words of love,*
> *Make this world an Eden like the heaven above.*

TWO GLASSES OF MILK

I came across an old newspaper clipping in my files. It contained a story related by Bruce Prestidge, TFC Executive Director, but a google search did not produce a satisfactory candidate for which organization that was. Having no reason to doubt the story, and since it illustrates the type of kindness needed today, I'll share it with you.

One hot summer day a certain man's automobile broke down in an isolated area of a rural countryside. After walking for several miles the man came to a run-down farm house and saw a little girl playing outside. He approached the edge of the yard, caught the little girl's attention and called to her, "Could you please give me a drink of water, I'm very thirsty?" "We don't have any water in the house right now," the little girl responded, "but I can get you a glass of milk if that would be alright." The man nodded his head and the little girl brought him the glass of milk and then asked if he would like another. The man said he needed one more glass. After finishing the second glass of milk the man walked into town and got the assistance he needed to get his car repaired.

A few years later the little girl became desperately ill and was taken to a large city hospital for tests. The diagnosis was that she needed immediate surgery in order to live. Not having much money, her parents agonized over the cost of such an operation. They had no choice but to have it done. (Apparently there was no universal health care at that time or place.)

The surgery went well and soon the little girl was at home again. Shortly after she returned home the bill from the hospital came. Her parents opened the letter with dread, knowing that it would take them years to pay. Inside the envelope was a brief note that read, "Paid in full with two glasses of milk." The note was signed by the surgeon whose car had broken down that hot summer day.

Sow seeds of kindness to reap a harvest of love.

THEME 12

Nature

Some lessons can we learn from nature.

*"When I consider your heavens, the work of your fingers,
the moon and the stars, which you have set in place,
what is mankind that you are mindful of them,
human beings that you care for them?" Psalm 8:3-4*

UNIQUE DELIVERY SERVICE

Recent news casts have included stories about our postal delivery system and stolen parcels off the porches when packages have been left there. I have not had that happen to me. But I do know about an excellent transport system I use every day!

A. It includes about 120,000 km of pathways.

B. It delivers life-sustaining nutrients.

C. It picks up garbage on the same trip in the same vehicle.

D. It serves about 60,000,000,000 customers, daily.

E. About 1,200,000 "vehicles" wear out every second, after having made about 75,000 round trips during the 120 days of their "lives", and these vehicles are immediately fully replaced.

The answer is our bloodstream, an incredibly well-designed delivery and retrieval system. Wikipedia claims that 2.4 million red blood corpuscles (the vehicles) are recycled and replaced, from the bone marrow factory, every second (others put it at 1.2M). That is unbelievably amazing until you realize that there are over five million red cells in a microliter. A microliter is one millionth of a liter (a drop?). Blood is made up of red cells, white cells, platelets and soluble items like enzymes, sugar, salt, cholesterol, fats and plasma that requires water to maintain liquidity. There are actually two circulatory systems. The pulmonary system pumps used blood to the lungs for releasing carbon dioxide and absorbing oxygen. The systemic one receives oxygen enriched blood from the lungs and pumps it out to the body. As the heart pumps the blood through the network, these very, very tiny red cells reach the capillaries, fold and twist to make it into and through those tiny passages. Their flexible, oval, biconcave shape makes this possible (did this shape happen by chance?). There they unload oxygen and nutrients into the cells (customers) and pick up carbon dioxide and other wastes.

Should a cut or tear cause bleeding, platelets will be rushed to the location (do they have GPS?) in seconds to create a temporary patch. Then our body will use raw materials stored up for this purpose to make fibrin for complete healing.

Should disease or infections invade, antibodies will be dispatched that will fight to the death. Medicines aid that battle too. Much more could be said about this incredible system. What is our part in this? Eat healthy foods, drink enough clean water, exercise daily and monitor blood pressure. This marvelous system created for us will then serve us well.

WOW!!

BRAVE SQUIRREL

I was waiting for a friend at the corner of Tucelnuit Dr. and Eastside Ave. in Oliver, B.C., when I spotted a squirrel making his way along the overhead power line crossing Eastside Ave. The wind was making it a bit difficult but then two crows added to the problem. One perched a few feet in front of the squirrel and the other one a few feet behind. The squirrel stopped for a while, battling the swaying wire and pondering the next move. It was a long, uninviting jump down to the pavement. The squirrel must have concluded there was only one way to go and that was forward no matter what. As (s)he moved forward the crow hopped a few feet forward too. This kept happening until the brave squirrel reached the other pole.

Have you ever felt trapped? There seemed to be no way out. When circumstances in life block our path with overwhelming odds against us, it may just be that we need to move ahead with courage and faith in the God who cares.

WATER, WATER EVERYWHERE!

We hear a lot about water in the news. Too much water and we get floods that cause horrible damage. Too little and there's drought, fires and famine. We need the right amount of precipitation for plant growth and animal thirst. Some of the rain needs to filter through the ground to be cleansed, absorb mineral nutrients and then sustain the water table. Surface water provides evaporation. Condensation happens in the atmosphere as water vapor condenses into clouds that spread rain. Then the cycle continues. What a marvelous, automatic system powered by the sun that just happens to be the right distance away.

A second wonder is happening whether we realize it or not. The root hairs on the roots of plants absorb water from the ground by osmosis. Then capillary action causes the water to rise up the tree trunk, limbs and twigs through tiny capillary tubes to reach every leaf, blossom or fruit. Capillary action happens because the polarized water molecule 'climbs' up the capillary tube as it is drawn to the molecules of the capillary wall. A huge tree can draw tons of water hundreds of feet straight up. In the leaves the process of photosynthesis produces food, transpires oxygen into the air for us and expels some water vapor. Eventually this helps clouds form, precipitation results and the cycle keeps going. It is all there to enable life to survive. It was created that way for us and all the plants and animals. Amazing!!

Gratefulness for that will help to keep us on the sunny side.

NOW THAT'S COMMITMENT!

In his book of true illustrations, Ivor Powell tells of an acquaintance in South Africa who was compelled to stop at the side of the road because a dove refused to move out of the way. Upon inspection he noticed that the dove was standing next to its dead mate, undoubtedly killed by another car. Approaching close to the bird still didn't cause it to leave. He finally picked it up, gently stroked it and threw it up into the air. It circled the area and then returned to its post beside the dead mate. Several times the man repeated his efforts to get the dove to leave permanently, but to no avail.

Later that day, on his return trip, the driver spotted two dead doves at that same spot, probably killed by a driver who expected the dove to escape in time. What could possibly be the sunny side of this story? It's a very sad story. It's enough to make you cry! Nobody would ever die for me. But wait! What about Good Friday? Crucifixion! Somebody did die for me!

Both accounts herald devotion and faithfulness to a cause. They also make us think of health care workers and caregivers who give up a lot to support those with severely debilitating illnesses at home or in Care Facilities. It must be very emotionally draining to work with someone like that for a long time, only to see them slip away. We applaud that faithful commitment.

EAGLE'S NEST

A tall tree or a high mountain ledge is often the site of an eagle's nest. The first layer of the nest contains thorny branches, sharp objects and perhaps even some jagged stones. This seems to label the bird as somewhat stupid, but wait! She covers these with fur from animals, soft materials she has found and even some of her own feathers or down. It becomes a very comfortable place for the eaglets when they hatch.

As the hatchlings grow the nest becomes crowded but still very comfortable. And they get meals on wings regularly. Why leave the nest? So the mother begins to stir up the nest. With her talons she throws out the soft stuff bit by bit. The nest becomes less comfortable. Deliveries of food may become more sporadic adding to the distress of the young birds. Eventually the motivation to leave the nest and fend for themselves becomes strong enough to launch the eaglets into flight. The mother's actions were not cruel or selfish but necessary to produce maturity.

Deuteronomy 32:11 says, *"As an eagle stirs up her nest..."* Has the Lord been urging you or me to leave our comfort zones and launch out into action? Perhaps the idea is frightening and we object to the discomfort but the Lord wants us to spread our wings of faith and venture into what could be risky or uncomfortable work for Him.

The sunny side is not always the comfortable side.

LIKE AN EAGLE

Is the following an unbelievable, outrageous claim??

Isaiah 40:31 *"...but those who hope in the LORD will renew their strength. They will soar on wings like eagles; they will run and not grow weary, they will walk and not be faint."*

That seems like an unattainable goal. How could we ever be like that? However, as a metaphor for spiritual victories we can experience those heights. We are called to fly like an eagle and run like an athlete. Unfortunately, not all Christians attain those heights.

Suppose we focus on just some of the characteristics of an eagle? What are the implications for us?

1. Eagles can fly high, up to 8000 feet. Flying high is often a picture of being able to rise above circumstances.
2. Eagles are solitary except when with a mate. They are faithful to that mate. The implication is obvious.
3. They see clearly and far. It is said that an eagle can spot an ant from the 10th story of a building. It helps a lot if we can clearly see where a certain course of action will take us. Leaders see farther ahead and more clearly.
4. Their vision is well protected. There is both an inner and outer eyelid. The inner one will allow them to see quite well. It is enough of a 'sunglass' to protect them from retinal damage by sunlight. The outer eyelid covers completely. We will never be without the need for protection from harmful influences.
5. While most predators avoid snakes an eagle is not intimidated by them. They become a food source for them. It's great when an obstacle or sinful act can be transformed into a beneficial one.

Fly like an eagle!

FIGHTING AT THE FEEDER

The goldfinches are fighting at the feeder. Even though there are six perches on the feeder and more than enough seed for all of them, they fight. One finch seems to be the boss, chasing others away when they try to get some of the seeds.

I feel like capturing that little stinker and keeping him off the feeder while the others get their share, but what would happen is that another one of them would simply declare himself in charge and do the same thing. I could go over there and try to explain that it is foolish for them to fight but they would just retreat to the top of the tree and wait for me to leave. I could shout and rail at them but then they would fly away.

Now if I could become a goldfinch while still retaining my insight I could communicate to them. I could explain that there is enough for them all and fighting ruins things. I might convince them that the people in this house want to provide for them and enjoy them. Let's just share and get along and we'll all be happy.

Come to think of it, that's what God had to do for us. He became a man in the person of Jesus Christ to tell us that God loves us, wants to provide for us and enjoy a relationship with us. More than that, He wants to forgive us, give us new life and bring us into His family. There is enough in this world for all of us yet in our families, our communities, our countries and in our world we fight over possessions and power.

Fighting doesn't fit the sunny side.

LEARNING TO FLY

In the tree just outside our window a pair of crows built a nest. For weeks the crows brought food for the baby crows. It seemed as though it wasn't just the parents that fed the baby crows, others joined in for the task. Eventually the young crows were able to hop out of the nest but one of them was reluctant to try flying. For days it would step out onto a branch but go no further. It would try flying from one branch to another but no more in spite of urging from adult crows. That illustrated a lesson for me. I was meant to be and do what a maturing, growing Christian should be doing. Yet so often I was reluctant to step out in faith. It seemed too risky in spite of being challenged to venture out.

Then one day there was a commotion outside the window. The young crow flew from one tree to the next. Then back again. Loudly it trumpeted (rather hoarse trumpet) its success. Not long after that it was out there doing what crows do. That included 'choir practice' at about five a.m. Why would they need a rehearsal when they've only got a few croaks in their repertoire? However, they are one of the more intelligent birds. Their actions can teach us something. Take courage and venture beyond your comfort zone.

BIRTH OF A GIRAFFE

The birth of a giraffe is very different from most other animal births. After a 14 month pregnancy the mother giraffe will remain standing even though she knows that birth is beginning to happen. The process usually takes anywhere from 30 minutes to two hours. We would think that the mother would lie down, but she doesn't. When the baby calf emerges it will drop 6 or more feet, landing on its two front feet and the head. What a mean way to enter life in this world! After rolling onto its back it will stay there for a few minutes while the mother begins the clean-up process. She will also stand over it and check the area for predators.

This is when disturbing actions by the mother will begin to take place if the calf does not get up right way. She will nudge it and then give it a solid kick if it does not get up. The calf will try, very awkwardly, and often seem to give up. Then the mother will give it another kick. This action is repeated until the calf is standing. At this point the mother may knock it down again, and again, until the calf has learned to get up and stay up. The reason is clear. The most vulnerable time for mother and calf is during, and right after, birthing. The calf must learn to run, not just stand or walk, if it is to stay alive. All this has to happen the first day. What an introduction to life and death for a newborn giraffe!

We were not dealt with that way as infants but life has its ways of knocking us about throughout our days and years. Mark them down as learning experiences. They are opportunities to develop survival skills.

LEMMINGS

Lemmings are prolific little rodents, living mostly in Sweden and Norway. They are about the size of a field mouse and live on vegetation. Twice a year they raise a brood of from five to eight. That means a huge population explosion will develop. About every four years something causes them to head for the ocean. Some may take months or even more than a year to get there, some die on the way. Of those who do arrive at the ocean, many will plunge into the sea and drown.

Widespread is the idea that the lemmings are driven to suicide by a built in drive to reduce the population. Apparently, this is not the case. Food shortage does drive them to seek better pastures, since they are vegetarian. They are also capable swimmers and may 'dream' of better things across the water. When it is the ocean they plunge into none of them succeed. It's a dream that became a nightmare.

On occasion I have detected a valid, innate urge to seek something more fulfilling, more meaningful, more satisfying to my hunger for significance. But I have also sought them where they cannot be found. Meaning and significance in life is bound up in our relationships. If genuine, helpful relationships are missing we will seek fulfillment in unfruitful places, and maybe 'drown'. The positive point is that even if all else fails, we can be sure that God loves each one of us and can direct us to goals that will be satisfying and meaningful.

May you be blessed with good relationships.

LIMPET TEETH

Mankind has learned to combine strength and flexibility by making composite materials. We put steel bars in concrete and fibreglass into plastics. But we weren't the first to do that. A limpet is able to cling to rocks using the suction of a muscular foot and the adhesiveness of mucous. As it moves slowly along, its tongue (radula) can scrape algae off the rocks to use as food. Its tongue is covered with tiny teeth made of the strongest biological material known, geothite. It uses iron oxide and hydroxide to form geothite whose fibres are 1000 times thinner than the glass fibres in fibreglass. This microscopic size helps to defy cracks or flaws in the teeth.

Professor A. Barber was moved to write the following comment.

> *Biology is a great source of inspiration as an engineer. These (limpet) teeth are made up of very small fibres, put together in a particular way and we should be thinking of making our own structures following the same design principles.*

Good idea! It is fitting that we applaud the inventor who used what was already there, but how can we then ignore the Creator who made what is there in the first place?

Professor A. Barber, Journal of Royal Science, Feb. 18, 2015

MANTA RAYS

Robotics engineers have tried to copy the design of some aquatic creatures in order to produce efficient underwater robots. This bio-mimetic branch of research has recently been targeting the manta ray for study because it has everything you would want in an AUV, (autonomous underwater vehicle). The manta's wing-like fin not only flaps up and down but also undulates, sending a traveling wave from the front to the rear of the wing. This undulatory part of the swimming is really the most important. It supplies 4 times as much propulsive power as flapping the wing. Furthermore, the challenge to mimic its movement is incredibly more challenging than they thought. Topline researchers, multiple universities and multi-million dollar research grants have so far made little progress toward a flexible manta-like wing that can be controlled accurately.

How is it that many of these same researchers who are addressing the project with high intelligence, finances and technology will claim that the manta ray evolved by chance mutations and natural selection with no intelligent design behind it? That would make it just an accident. That cannot be!! There is a very, very Intelligent Creator behind the design. We are accountable to Him.

Source: D. Catchpoole's article in Creation magazine, Vol. 38, No. 3, 2016

We are an even more complex creation than the manta ray!

MONARCH BUTTERFLY

Walking along the hike & bike trail a person may well spot a green-striped worm feeding on the milkweed if it's that certain time of the year. Repulsive, it seems. That ugly, chewing machine seems to be destructive and greedy. It hatched out of an egg attached conveniently to the underside of the milkweed plant. After being protected by the milkweed it is now eating its host. How ungrateful.

Then in fall the worm builds itself a sort of 'coffin', called a chrysalis, and attaches it to a twig for the winter. During that winter the worm disintegrates, almost liquefies, into a formless mass and transforms into something that emerges in spring as the beautiful Monarch Butterfly. You'd have to see that whole process happening in order to really be convinced, I'd say. What a change!!

That kind of physical transformation doesn't happen to us as we grow but it can happen spiritually inside of us. We are promised in Paul's letter to the Corinthians that *"If anyone is in Christ he is a new creation..."*

It's wonderful to have that potential offered to us.

OPEN FOR BUSINESS

The tulips are blooming. During the day the petals open up, displaying their beauty and attracting pollinating insects. They are open for business. When darkness falls the petals close up the flower. They conserve their fragrance when there's no one to appreciate or use it. They display their beauty when there is someone to be attracted by it. That is an amazing design feature found in a number of plants. Furthermore that action must prevent unwelcome night guests and even avoid damage to an open flower at the wrong time. Tulips bloom such a short time that they have to capitalize on the best opportunities.

What is it that triggers those responses? It is the sunshine. I noticed that those tulips which were already exposed to the morning sun had opened up, those in the shade were still closed up. That sends a message to us. If we allow the sunshine (Sonshine?) of God's love to impact us we too can spread fragrance at the right time and draw people into positive experiences. It's darkness in our life that closes off communication and repels people. What kind of an aroma do I spread? What do I do with great opportunities for doing something good? Probing thought. Open up to the Son shine!

PEACE

(When times of transition or crisis occur many resort to a familiar place of refuge where they can go to get their thoughts together and regain perspective in life. For me this place was a tree overhanging a creek and curved in such a way as to form a moss-covered 'lazyboy chair' above the water on the Abbotsford acreage we were selling. Big changes were ahead for us. On the last Sunday afternoon of our residence there, I resorted to that tree one more time and wrote most of the following.)

It's quiet here couched in the crook of this overhanging tree.

> The creek beneath me gurgles its charm

> while the sun filters through the leaves.

> Birds ripple the stillness with their warble.

> It's so peaceful.

Why can't it stay like this?

Why does it have to change?

> Sometimes the storm rages, tearing clods from the bank or

>> gouging furrows with splintered trees.

> Sometimes a hawk claws the life out of a rodent,

>> it's my life or yours.

> Sometimes a fish gasps its last,

>> mercilessly plucked from its home.

> Sometimes the wind slices the air with sleet,

>> stripping the trees, gaunt ghosts of a fruitful past.

> Sometimes it's the dry season,

>> child of the same rays that warmed my mossy couch

now leach the last life out of the dry creek bed.

How much like life!

The virtuous and the violent,

the life-giving and the life-taking,

the warmth and the cold,

the pleasant and the harsh,

all wrapped in one bundle.

How much like death!

The bright and the beautiful so easily snatched away,

so quickly reversed,

so overwhelmingly harsh.

Why is there pleasure and pain? God has ordained both.

Out of adversity and struggle are born the delights of peace.

But now it's quiet here,

couched in the crook of this overhanging tree.

The creek still gurgles its charm,

the birds still warble their delight,

and I am at peace.

Written by Henry Wiebe, May,1992

FAMILY FINDS REFUGE

A family of 14 moved into our back yard a few days ago. The 12 "children" were hatched in the back yard of Len and Liz Darnbrough, just a few houses away from ours in Sunningdale, Oliver, BC. Maybe Ma and Pa Quail were the ones who had been invading Helen's garden earlier in spring. She replanted the carrots three times. They must have thought this place is Paradise, The Garden of Helen! So here were 12 little balls of fluff scurrying around after Ma Quail just one day after hatching. Must have been already learning how to find food for themselves. Pa Quail was on a fencepost, and vigorously sounded the alarm when I approached the garden. All twelve immediately obeyed Pa. Ma hid them all under the raspberry bushes. How did they know what to do? It's programmed into their DNA.

The whole process was a sight to behold. It took the edge off the frustrated feelings we had toward the parent quails for gobbling up the carrot shoots. Sadly, less than half of the chicks will live to adulthood. Tough, really tough! The next day the "family" came back with nine chicks. Obviously the Creator knew what He was doing when he gave quails the potential for twelve chicks two times a year and grizzly bears only one, and that not even every year.

Today the quail seemed to have moved on to someone else's yard. We'll kind of miss them but we'll still put the netting above the strawberries and peas next spring.

Those little chicks really brought on a sunny smile.

RIPENING FRUIT

Harvest time! What a great time of year as we reap the benefits of work and God's provision of ripening fruit. We are aware that most unripened fruit is inedible, even bitter. Certain varieties of persimmon don't sweeten until frost hits them. For other kinds of fruit the frost would ruin it and cause it to rot. If we liken the frost to adversities in life, the effect on us will be determined by what we are made of.

It's possible to go through life like an unripened fruit, unpleasant and bitter, refusing to let frosty experiences improve our character. Or we can let adversity be the change agent. If we get the cold shoulder, a frosty experience hits us, we can choose to sweeten under its influence or let it damage and decay us. Adversity can be a character building experience or take us down into despair. It depends on what we are made of.

We cannot avoid adversity, disappointments and trouble. We can choose to grow instead of rot under its influence.

SHEEP

Of all the millions of animals that exist on our planet, the Scriptures compare people most often to sheep. Psalm 23, likely the most well-known biblical poem, starts by saying *"The Lord is my shepherd..."* Isaiah 53 includes a reference to this comparison when it states: *"All we like sheep have gone astray..."*

Why would that be the choice? Sheep are generally recognized as being likely the most helpless, dependent, defenseless, straying, and confused animal on the planet. We prefer to think of ourselves as independent, capable, smart, strong and wise. In some ways we are but when it comes to moral anchors, spiritual battles and direction in life we too often fit the previous description.

On a positive note, sheep can be very trusting and very loyal. They sense when they have a shepherd who cares about them and will even sacrifice his own safety to protect them. He may even know them by name. He loves the sheep in spite of their straying ways. That's why Jesus is called the great shepherd of the sheep. He knows everything about us but loves us anyway.

It's a privilege to be one of His sheep.

THEME 13

Priorities

Do I have priorities in my life
whether I realize it or not?

"The most important one," answered Jesus, "is this: 'Hear, O Israel:
The Lord our God, the Lord is one. Love the Lord your God with all
your heart and with all your soul and with all your mind and with
all your strength.' The second is this: 'Love your neighbor as yourself.'
There is no commandment greater than these." Mark 12:29-31

BASIC QUESTIONS OF LIFE

I realize that some people rarely think about crucial philosophical issues in life. Yet, the five most frequently asked questions of life are probably like the five W's of investigative journalism: who, what, when, where and why.

1. Where did I come from and how did I get here?
2. Why am I here?
3. What went wrong with this world?
4. Who is going to fix it?
5. When I die what happens to me?

I am personally convinced that the following are brief but good answers, although I know there are those who will disagree.

1. We have a **Creator to believe in Who** tells us we were designed and made by the One who owns the universe. He cares a lot about each one of us.
2. We have a **cause to live for** as we proclaim Jesus Christ to be the Way, the Truth and the Life. That's **Why** we are here. This relationship can lead to a joy-filled life because He wants us to live life to the full.
3. We have a **creed to live by** since He told us that to love God and people are the two most important principles of life. **What's** wrong is that this is ignored by many.
4. We have a **conscience to live with** that can be cleared of guilt because there is forgiveness. This is foundational to spiritual and mental health. We also have a **community to live in Where** we experience the support and fellowship of others and give the same to them. This is essential for relational health. Jesus is the One **Who** can fix this since He has paid the penalty for sin.

5. We have a **consummation to look forward to When** we
   die. We await the time when those who have put their trust
   in Him will be with the Lord forever.

The prospects are bright on the sunny side.

HATTIE'S GIFT

Giving gifts is a commendable practice upheld by many. What do
you think of Hattie's gift?

Hattie May Wiatt wanted to go to Sunday School. She went to a
small nearby church and asked if she could come. They told her
that the classes were full and there was just no room for more. She
returned to her home a disappointed girl, but understood the reason.

About two years later she died. Under her pillow was found an
old, torn pocketbook. Inside was a scrap of paper in which she had
wrapped 57 pennies. Scrawled on the paper in a childish hand were
the words: *"To help build the church a little bigger so that more children
can go there for Sunday School."*

Deeply touched, the pastor told the congregation about Hattie's gift.
The newspaper published the story and soon gifts poured in from far
and wide. The fund grew to about $250,000. A bigger church build-
ing was erected, Temple Baptist Church in Philadelphia, which grew
to seat 3000 people. Small gift from a little girl – big results. (Source:
Encyclopedia of 7700 Illustrations by Paul l. Tan, #1833)

We never know what a small act of kindness with the right motive
can accomplish.

LAMB'S CRY

A group of tourists were visiting a sheep farm in Australia at shearing time. Hundreds of sheep were in an enclosure awaiting their turn to be shorn. The tour guide decided to demonstrate the remarkable ability of a mother sheep to detect the cry of its own lamb. The guide placed a little lamb on the opposite corner of the enclosure from where the mother was. For a while the lamb stood still. Then it realized that it was separated from its mother. It began to let out a weak but distressed 'baa'. Amidst the shouting of the shearers, the bleating of hundreds of other sheep and the noise of the shears the mother immediately picked up the lamb's cry and pushed her way through the herd to find the lamb.

Ever wonder how God can possibly notice our cry for help? We are told that He is ready to listen, willing to help and able to deliver any of His 'children' even when lost among the more than seven billion people on earth.

Help is a cry away.

MAKING MONEY

In 1923 at the Edgewater Beach Hotel in Chicago, some of the world's greatest business leaders and financiers met to discuss mutual interests. Among them were the following men who **at that time** occupied these stated positions: Charles Schwab, president of the largest independent steel company; Samuel Insull, president of the greatest utility company; Howard Hopson, president of the largest gas company; Arthur Cutton, the greatest wheat speculator; Richard Whitney, president of the New York Stock Exchange; Albert Fall, member of the U.S. president's cabinet; Jesse Livermore, greatest 'bear' on Wall St.; Ivar Krueger, head of the greatest business monopoly; and Leon Fraser, president of the Bank of International Settlement.

In 1948 research was conducted to see how these same men had fared after 25 years.

Charles Schwab lived on borrowed money for 5 years before dying penniless.

Samuel Insull died a fugitive from justice and penniless in a foreign land.

Howard Hopson became insane.

Arthur Cutton died abroad insolvent.

Richard Whitney had recently been released from Sing Sing Penitentiary.

Albert Fall was pardoned from prison so he could die at home.

Jesse Livermore, Ivar Krueger and Leon Fraser had all committed suicide.

"Do not let the good things of life rob you of the best things." M.D. Babcock

THE OLD MAN OF THE MOUNTAIN

In the mountains of northern New Hampshire lies Profile Lake. For decades people have made their way to its shore so that from a certain spot they can look 1200 feet up the mountainside to see the shape of a man's head. It's a huge rock outcropping jutting out from the side of Profile Mountain. That shape was carved out of the red granite by storms, water and freezing temperatures. The outcropping was the size of a 4 story building.

People living in the area became attached to it. It was almost as though they got comfort from that idea that someone seemed to constantly be watching over them. The Old Man of the Mountain would always be there for them. Tourists came to see it. Daniel Webster wrote about it. Nathanial Hawthorne authored a book about it called *The Great Stone Face*. In 1939 a thirteen year old boy, Robert Doane, wrote a poem about it in which he said:

"It was made from a mountain of granite with the skill of a sculptor's hand, And guards the green valley below it as time passes over the land."

Time did pass and on May 3, 2003 the forces of nature carved one crack too many and the huge, great stone face came crashing down. There was a sense of deep loss from some of the residents. It was as though there would now be no one watching over them. But that is not the case. Centuries ago the psalmist wrote:

I lift my eyes up to the hills – where does my help come from? My help comes from the Lord, the Maker of heaven and earth. He will not let your foot slip – he who watches over you will not slumber.

He concludes Psalm 121 with: *"...the Lord will watch over your coming and going both now and forevermore."*

This is a Guard you can depend on. He will not come crashing down. Place your faith in the Lord.

IS IT NAILED DOWN?

Nails in the right place, good nails, hold things together. Nails in the wrong place can tear you apart, or poor nails fail you. Nails can teach us a lot. The Bible speaks of "a nail in a sure place" in Isaiah 22:23, namely a nail that could be depended on. Two verses later it talks about that nail being sheared off, resulting in ruin. Do you have things nailed down right? Is your nail dependable? In order to be useful that nail would have to measure up in at least five ways.

1. **Straight** - we don't want to use crooked nails. In life we appreciate the integrity of one who is tried and true. Prov.3:6 says, *"Trust in the Lord with all your heart and do not lean on your own understanding. In all your ways acknowledge Him and He will make your paths **straight**."*

2. **Strong** - we wouldn't use a toothpick for a nail. "Be **strong** in the Lord" we are told in Ephesians 6:10. Our society today desperately needs people who are prepared to stand firm on principles.

3. **Sharp** – in most cases nails have sharp points to make it easier to penetrate the wood. We are told in Hebrews 4:12 that *"the word of God is **sharp** and powerful"*. It has the ability to penetrate our thoughts and also discern what is right. It can cut through the confusion and make things clear. We need the focused direction that God's Word gives.

4. **Solid** - ever tried nailing into jello? A nail will do us no good unless it is driven into something solid. Life without a solid foundation is the ultimate insecurity. 2 Timothy 2:19 reminds us that God's **solid foundation** stands firm. What am I, or you, using as the basis for life?

5. **Struck** - no matter how straight, strong or sharp the nail is, or how solid the wood behind it is, no good will be accomplished until it has been struck. Ultimately, that struck nail in a sure place is a picture of the Lord Jesus Christ. It tells us in Isaiah 53:8 *"for the transgression of my people he was **stricken**"*. The judgment of God for sin fell on Him when He hung on the cross. Now we have the opportunity to go free and forgiven.

If you admit that you are a sinner in need of forgiveness, the Lord will grant you the free gift of salvation. If we refuse to repent and reject Jesus as Savior, ignoring the fact that sin needs to be dealt with, the free gift of salvation will not be ours. **Place your confidence on the nail in a sure place?** It'll bring it all together for you.

THE TOUCH OF THE MASTER'S HAND

'Twas battered and scarred, and the auctioneer thought it hardly
worth his while
to waste his time on the old violin, but he held it up with a smile.

"What am I bid, good people", he cried, "Who starts the bidding
for me?"
"One dollar, one dollar, do I hear two?" "Two dollars, who makes
it three?"
"Three dollars once, three dollars twice, going for three…"

But, No!
From the room far back a gray bearded man came forward and
picked up the bow.
Then wiping the dust from the old violin and tightening up
the strings,
he played a melody, pure and sweet, as sweet as the angel sings.

The music ceased and the auctioneer with a voice that was quiet
and low
said, "What now am I bid for this old violin?",
as he held it aloft with its bow.

"One thousand, one thousand, do I hear two?" "Two thousand,
who makes it three?"
"Three thousand once, three thousand
twice. Going and gone", said he.

The audience cheered, but some of them cried, "We just
don't understand."

"What changed its worth?" Swift came the reply.
"The Touch of the Masters Hand."

"And many a man with life out of tune all battered and bruised
with sin
is auctioned cheap to a thoughtless crowd much like that old violin.

A mess of pottage, too much wine, a game and he travels on.
He is going once, he is going twice, he is going and almost gone.

But the Master comes, and the foolish crowd never can
quite understand, the worth of a soul and the change
that is wrought by the Touch of the Masters' Hand.

Myra Brooks Welch 1921 La Verne, Calif.

REFUGE

A large evergreen tree stood not far from our home in Oliver, BC. We could watch the antics of birds on that tree from our kitchen window. Often several birds sat on the very tips near the top of the tree to scout out the scenery or watch for predators. Sometimes there was a whole flock of birds in or on the tree having an exuberant choir practice. Occasionally there would be a bemused dove on the very top watching little birds chase each other like kids on a playground. Sometimes I saw a small bird in full flight dive into the depths of the tree. Why would the bird do that? Could it be simply overjoyed to come home? Could it be that a hawk was chasing it and it was frantic about finding a safe place?

We experience the same range of emotions in our life. Sometimes we wonder at the beauty around us, sometimes there is joyful celebration, sometimes a dash for safety. At such times we can rely on the One who really cares about us. As the psalmist put it: *"Trust in him at all times, O people, pour out your hearts to him, for God is our refuge." Psalm 62:8*

SECOND FIDDLE

The conductor of a prominent orchestra was once asked, "What is the most difficult instrument to play in the orchestra?" He replied, "The hardest instrument to play is second fiddle." Playing the support role for someone else who is getting the majority of the recognition is not an easy task. Rejoicing in someone else's success when you've had a part in producing that is difficult. Most people would want to be in first place. Few are willing to remain unrecognized and still be diligent in performing well. There are those who play a strong supportive role on a sports team but the star players get most of the credit. Background volunteers in many organizations, including the church, serve important roles but the public figure gets the acclaim. Playing 'second fiddle' in any aspect of life is a special challenge.

This makes it particularly meaningful when we are told in Philippians 2:7 in the New Testament that Christ "*...made Himself nothing, taking the very nature of a servant...*" This was the King of the Universe serving in menial ways. This was the completely innocent Messiah taking the extreme punishment for sins He did not commit. We, all mankind, were to blame. It showed how very much He loved each one of us.

Love thrives on the sunny side.

THEME 14

Rescue

Are we grateful or humiliated when we realize that we need rescuing?

"Guard my life and rescue me; do not let me be put to shame, for I take refuge in you." Psalm 25:20

AVALANCHE

Only 35 kilometers to go. After three weeks of working at a remote lodge they'd soon be back home in Terrace, B.C. Rounding a curve in a driving rain the car skidded to an abrupt stop in ankle deep mud and rocks. Mudslide! Efforts to back out were in vain. Then the roar of more water, logs, stumps and boulders screamed at them to run but it was too late. The August, 2004, mudslide caught Allen Jones, Michael Williams and Jenny Parnell in its merciless torrent. Travelers caught on both sides of the 175 meter slide slogged into the mess to pull, wrench and pry the three of them from the mud that swallowed them and the debris that pinned them down. That group included paramedics from an ambulance that was also blocked. Airlifted into town, they survived due to the valiant rescue work of willing people.

Sometimes we feel as though life has served up a deluge of trouble for us too. We are overwhelmed! There seems to be no way to dig our way out. It's then that the Lord's invitation to call upon Him in the day of trouble gives hope for deliverance. He can help us break through the mess. He does care when we hurt.

BATTLING EBOLA

The heart of Kent Brantly's goal was to be involved in medical missions. His first stint in a "third world" country was Liberia in 2003. After marriage in 2008 his wife, Amber, joined him in such ventures. When the Ebola crisis broke out in Africa it spread to become one of the most devastating medical crises known. Instead of running away, Dr. Brantly stayed to help the suffering people. The risk was high. In the summer of 2014, three days after sending his wife and family to the U.S.A., he was diagnosed as having contracted the virus himself. The World Medical Mission and Samaritan's Purse, with whom he was serving, sprang into action to somehow get him back to the

U.S.A. in an effort to save his life. The only plane they could enlist flew him part way across the Atlantic but had to turn back because they were losing air pressure in the cabin. Upon landing back in Liberia the mission staff were desperate for answers. They were in a position where they could do nothing but watch him die. At this point someone arrived from Sierra Leone with a box containing an untried and unauthorized serum. It had only been tried on animals (including monkeys) but not humans, and the medical people in Sierra Leone were not willing to use it on people. In the Liberia mission the staff decided to trust the Lord and use it since the alternate was to just let Dr. Brantly die. Prayer had been frequent and fervent. Upon injection his body went into convulsions. Panic stricken they were relieved to find out that this had happened to the monkeys too. The convulsions soon ended. In about 30 minutes the whole scene changed. Dr. Brantly was able to get up and use the washroom. He was now well enough to be flown to Emory Hospital in Atlanta where he, and a nurse who had also contracted Ebola, did recover.

If the plane had not been turned back he would likely have died before arriving in the U.S.A. Even if he would have arrived alive, they would not have had the serum needed. Turning back had been seen as a terrible defeat but God knew better. It was the solution. Dr. Brantly is alive now, still serving needy people and giving all the credit to the Lord. Website search under his name, or Samaritan's Purse, will give you more details and also how you might be able to watch the movie made of the story. It is called *Facing Darkness*. Some websites omit the part about the use of the unauthorized serum.

God cares very much about you too.

CAN YOU SLEEP WHEN THE WIND BLOWS?

Years ago, a farmer who owned land along the Atlantic seacoast, advertised for hired hands. Most people were reluctant to work on farms along the Atlantic. They dreaded the awful storms that raged across the ocean, wreaking havoc on the buildings and crops. As the farmer interviewed applicants for the job, he received a steady stream of refusals.

Finally, a short, thin man, well past middle age, approached the farmer. "Are you a good farm hand?" the farmer asked him. "Well, I can sleep when the wind blows," answered the little man. Although puzzled by this answer, the farmer, desperate for help, hired him. The little man worked well around the farm, busy from dawn to dusk, and the farmer felt satisfied with the man's work. Then one night the wind howled loudly in from offshore.

Jumping out of bed, the farmer grabbed a lantern and rushed next door to the hired hand's sleeping quarters. He shook the little man and yelled, "Get up! A storm is coming! Tie things down before they blow away!" The little man rolled over in bed and said firmly, "No sir. I told you, I can sleep when the wind blows." Enraged by the response, the farmer was tempted to fire him on the spot. Instead, he hurried outside to prepare for the storm. To his amazement, he discovered that all of the haystacks had been covered with tarpaulins. The cows were in the barn, the chickens were in the coops, and the doors were barred. The shutters were tightly secured. Everything was tied down. Nothing could blow away. The farmer then understood what his hired hand meant, so he returned to his bed to also sleep while the wind blew.

When you're prepared spiritually, mentally, and physically you have nothing to fear. Can you sleep when the wind blows through your life? The hired hand in the story was able to sleep because he had secured the farm against the storm. We secure ourselves against the storms of life by grounding ourselves in the Word of God. We won't understand everything and control even fewer things. We just need to place our trust in Christ and practice His ways to have peace in the storms. I hope you enjoy your day and that you sleep well.

CATASTROPHES

We've heard a lot in the news about the destruction caused by floods, tornadoes, earthquakes and fires. The damage and dismay is overwhelming. We sympathise with all those affected. We are told that the very center of the tornado can be a place of quiet stillness. It is so hard to visualize winds of 150 km an hour whirling around such a calm refuge.

The storms of life will come too. They can be so destructive. Relationships crumble, finances disappear, health fails or friends move away. Is it possible to find any peace when such calamities come our way? While we don't have a simplistic solution we can have peace in the middle of it all. Jesus promised, *"Peace I leave with you; my peace I give you. I do not give to you as the world gives. Do not let your hearts be troubled and do not be afraid."* John 14:27

There is peace on the sunny side.

MYSTERIOUS WAYS

William Cowper was frequently troubled by feelings of despair and grief. In his deep depression one day he summoned a horse-drawn carriage (this was in the mid to later 1700's) to take him to one of the London bridges. His intention was to take a suicidal jump into the Thames. But just at that time one of the densest fogs ever blanketed the city. In the confusion the driver got lost and drove around for an hour trying to find the bridge. Disgusted, William decided to stop the 'taxi', get out and walk. When he got off he found himself to be back at his own house. The driver had travelled in a circle. Totally overwhelmed by this sudden surprise, he took it as an act of the restraining hand of God. Needless to say, he did not try suicide again. Instead he decided then and there to cast his burden on the Lord for resolution. He immediately sat down and penned the words to a hymn that still appears in many hymnals. The first two verses say:

> God moves in a mysterious way His wonders to perform;
> He plants His footsteps in the sea, and rides upon the storm.
> Ye fearful saints fresh courage take; the clouds ye so much dread
> Are big with mercy, and shall break in blessings on your head.

That kind of care and compassion from God still operates today.

RESCUING THE IMPORTANT

A theme has pervaded the reports and interviews arising out of the rash of fires around our country and in other places around the world. Although the devastation of losing property and personal belongings is very real and very stressful, a frequent response reveals several things that identify what really counts.

Family – the lives of family members figures high on the list. Even if much else is lost the value of family members surviving rises above it.

Friends – the care and help of friends who put themselves out for the unfortunate ones rates very high on the list of what was meaningful. The bonds of friendship are strong in times like this.

Memories – items we possess that cannot be replaced by money or insurance are often among the things rescued first. Life is so very much wrapped up in memories triggered by items we cherish.

It's almost as though the fire has burned away some of the hard feelings and bad memories we've harbored against others. We must not trivialize material loss, but perhaps this is a sunny side to tragedy.

FLEEING

Michael J. Petri of McIntosh, Minnesota reported the following incident in the summer of 1986.

> One evening a woman was driving home when she noticed a huge truck behind her that was driving uncomfortably close. She stepped on the gas to gain some distance from the truck, but when she sped up, the truck did too. The faster she drove, the faster the truck did.
>
> Now scared, she exited the freeway. But the truck stayed with her. The woman then turned up a main street, hoping to lose her pursuer in traffic. But the truck ran a red light and continued the chase.
>
> Reaching the point of panic, the woman whipped her car into a service station and bolted out of her auto screaming for help. The truck driver sprang from his truck and ran toward the car. Yanking the back door open, the driver pulled out a man hidden in the back seat.
>
> The woman was running from the wrong person. From his high vantage point, the truck driver had spotted a would-be rapist in the woman's car. The chase was not his effort to harm her but to save her even at the cost of his own safety.

Likewise, many people run from God, fearing what He might do to them. But His plans are for good not evil – to rescue us from the hidden (or not so hidden) sins that endanger our lives.

Jesus said, *"I am come that you might have life, and have it more abundantly."* John 10:10

WHY??

The Humboldt, Sk. crash of Apr. 6, 2018 has raised serious questions. If there is a God who is all-powerful, all-knowing and loving why did He let this happen? Couldn't He have somehow held up the semi-trailer by just two seconds and the bus would have passed in front of the truck? Couldn't He have caused a traffic delay for just a minute to hold the bus back? Why would so many innocent young men die because one driver didn't notice, didn't see or ignored a stop sign? The overwhelming grief of so many families and friends plus the devastated future of the seriously injured would have been avoided. On top of that we can only imagine the horrible effect on the truck driver's mind and life. We ache for him too.

But wait a minute? Do I know how often the Lord has stepped in to prevent a disaster in my life? Could it be that there are thousands of times every day in Canada when He has prevented serious accidents and we don't even know it? All this in spite of not heeding warnings about drug overdoses, alcoholism, distracted driving, war due to power struggles, corruption that ruins lives and many more evils? The consequences often kill innocent as well as guilty people? Yet, how many warnings signs in life have I (or we) ignored and God has been gracious?

Why did this horrible accident happen? Is God doing anything about the mess on this planet? Yes, He did. On the cross Jesus cried out, "My God! My God, why have You forsaken me?" It wasn't the physical torture and death that troubled Him. It was that *"...He bore our sins in His own body on the cross..."* 1 Peter 2:24 This means He took the rap for everybody who turns to Him, including what's listed above. That's a major act of forgiveness and grace.

We grieve along with many in the world for the Bronco community. I wish I had all the answers, but I don't. Instead, I will depend on those answers I can't question instead of questions I can't answer.

The Son is shining behind the dark clouds.

TRAPPED IN A STORM SEWER

For days in June, 1989, tropical storm Allison had drenched Houston, TX. Kept indoors for days, seven year old Latricia and her cousin, eight year old Krystal, pleaded with Karen Reese (Latricia's mom), "Can we go out and play?" Since the storm had abated significantly and other children were playing in the flooded street, Karen consented. After a while the two girls eyed a ditch with deeper, flowing water to wade in. That fun turned to horror when Latricia lost her footing and was swept away into a culvert. She disappeared! It wasn't a culvert that opened on the other side of a road. It emptied into a catch basin and from there a shaft led to the storm sewer system. A neighbor had seen Latricia disappear, called 911 while her husband sent Krystal to get the mother. The firemen, police and many volunteers rushed to the scene. They knew the water dropped down a three meter shaft into a one meter sewer pipe. Frantically the whole crew tore off manhole covers, searching the roiling water with poles, but to no avail. Maybe the water had taken her all the way into the bayou just blocks away. The three hour search in the bayou was called off at 10 pm. Darkness in more than one form enveloped them all. It was hopeless. A distraught mother clung to Latricia's picture and sobbed.

Meanwhile a terrified little girl had tumbled about like a rag doll as she bounced from one pipe system to another, nearly choking to death. Somehow her fingers latched onto a joint between two lengths of concrete pipe just as she lodged against some debris that stopped her disastrous hurtling. "Mommy, help me! Where am I?"

All through the night with the water thundering past her, Latricia hung on to her refuge. She pressed her head against the top of the pipe to breathe above the water, and prayed. When the water level dropped in the pitch dark pipe ants and mosquitoes were a problem. This was an excruciatingly horrible experience for a seven year old girl for 12 hours. She dared not lose her place. Her cries were desperate. As soon as it became light enough people joined the mother in a search which was now considered a recovery of the body. At about 7:30 a.m. Tim Gabrysch and Bardomiano Garcia came to check on water levels in the sewer system, unaware of the tragedy that had happened. Once informed they swung into action. Uncovering a manhole not far from the culvert Tim descended into the pipe system. He was surprised that the water level had reduced to less than 30 cm. Moving along with his flashlight he detected something about 30 meters down a pipe too small for him to enter. "Little girl, are you there?" Amazingly an answer came back, "Who are you? I want my mommy!" "Can you work your way to me and I'll take you to your mommy."

She came. Tim scooped her up, retraced his path and boosted her up to his partner. At the hospital the slight concussion, a banged-up ankle, and a bruised forehead plus her all night survival convinced Dr. Rodriguez that Someone had been watching out for her. Can you imagine the joy her mother experienced!

Based on the Reader's Digest, Oct., 1990 article
by P. Ola and E. D'Aulaire plus websites.

What if the two men had arrived hours or a day later? What if Latricia had not hung on? How terrible an ordeal for a small girl to be calling for mother in a storm sewer pipe when only God knows where she is. We've all likely complained about adversities. Why weren't others rescued? Three others drowned in that storm. Could it be that each one of us has been spared from disasters we didn't even know were facing us? Could it be that we repeatedly ignored God with not even a thank you for the basics of food, water and air plus the beauty and benefits of creation and then wondered why He doesn't listen to us?

MIND THE LIGHT

After many years of minding the lighthouse on Robbins Reef off the shores of the New England states, the keeper contracted pneumonia one cold, stormy night. His decades of faithful service now ended in death. His wife arranged for his body to be buried on the hillside shore of the mainland opposite the lighthouse. She then applied for, and received, the appointment to take his place as a keeper of the light. For 20 years she carried on alone. A New York City reporter came to the lighthouse for a visit and an interview before those 20 years were over. He asked her what motivated her to keep going alone for all the years. Her answer was: *"Every evening I stand at the door of the lighthouse and look across the waters to the hillside where my husband sleeps and I seem to hear his voice say with the same urgency as when he was alive, 'Mind the light! Mind the light!' This is what keeps me going."*

There are troubled waters, dark times and stormy events all around us too. I think of the children's song I learned many years ago.

This little light of mine, I'm gonna let it shine.

The community around us needs that. I am blessed by more than I deserve, and challenged by more than I can handle alone.

RESCUED FROM DROWNING

Crowds had gathered at the riverbank fairgrounds for the Lions Club music festival in Guyon, Quebec. The hot July, 1993 sun made the sandy beach an attraction too inviting to miss. Lonnie Collier, 15, Tera Mayhew, 14, and Scott Smith, 12, decided to walk 100 meters to where the Guyon River flowed into the Ottawa River. The warm shallow waters of the beach led to a sudden drop-off into the very cold current of the Ottawa River. The boys played the game of jumping into the cold current and experiencing the exhileration of swimming back into the warm water. This excitement turned into panic when the two boys jumped too far to battle the current back to shore. They were swept away.

Screams drew the attention of Dwight McMillan who ran over and dove into the current to rescue Scott. With great difficulty he managed to haul him back to safety. By then Lonnie was 60 meters away struggling to stay afloat. Though already exhausted, Dwight headed out for a second rescue attempt.

Upon reaching Lonnie the boy clutched at him in frenzied panic, clawing at Dwight and nearly causing the drowning of both of them. Repeated attempts to persuade Lonnie to relax so that he could be rescued failed. He sank out of sight. Darlene McMillan despaired when she saw Dwight disappear too. Meanwhile two men in a small boat were alerted to the trouble. When Dwight emerged with a limp Lonnie and no strength left the two men pulled alongside and brought them to shore. The two men said not a word as they brought them to shore. While the onlookers were pulling Dwight and Lonnie onto the beach, heaving and vomiting, the two men disappeared. Repeated efforts to locate them later failed. In Dec., 1994 Dwight was awarded the Governor Generals Medal of Bravery. In Feb., 1995 he received the Carnegie Hero Fund Commission.

But the two men who pulled Lonnie and Dwight out of the water and then disappeared are unheralded heroes of another kind.

Based on a March, 1996 report in Reader' Digest.

The three kids learned a lesson and perhaps someone will keep this story in mind when outdoor swimming weather approaches.

SURVIVING THE SIMILKAMEEN

Victor and Nadia Stankovic were on a June, 1982 early morning trip for a camper holiday in Penticton, B.C. A few kilometers past Manning Park they rounded a steep rock cliff that looked down on a full-torrent, pounding Similkameen River about ten meters below them. Just then one wheel hit a rock on the road, bouncing the vehicle out of control and catapulting it over the cliff. The camper rolled twice and landed upright in the middle of the raging river. The current began to carry it backward until it jammed on a huge boulder, with freezing water rushing into the cab. With great difficulty Victor managed to open one door slightly against the wild, 75 km/hr current so that they could squeeze through and reach the top of the camper. They were trapped. Any attempt to swim to shore would be suicidal.

A passing traveler saw them and phoned for help. Vacation-bound Norm Walker of the Canadian Coast Guard was flagged down. Park Rangers Peter Marochi and Peter Robinson were joined by RCMP Mark Oliver in seeking to help in the rescue effort as more than 50 passers-by watched. Even a stunned Mick Stankovic just happened to stop as he was passing through, only to find that it was his father and mother in the river. Someone urged Norm Lesage to bring his helicopter from where he was staying in a nearby cabin. Looking at the narrow passage-way between 30 meter lodgepole pines on either bank, he doubted his skills at performing a rescue. Victor and Nadia Stankovic's physical conditions were deteriorating. If rescue wasn't achieved soon they would likely be lost to the current. Rescue attempts by ropes nearly caused the drowning of Victor and Ranger Robinson. It would have to be the helicopter for Nadia. A very risky venture. A rescue harness was hastily fashioned as best they could and the two Rangers put their lives in jeopardy getting it to the camper. Three trips later, Lesage had successfully piloted the helicopter to bring all three off the camper. Five men: Walker, Robinson, Marochi, Oliver and Lesage, were awarded St. John Life Saving medals, RCMP Commendation for Bravery and the Governor General's Medal of Bravery. Well deserved!

Based on an article by Lynne Schuyler in the
April, 1985 issue of Reader's Digest.

It may well be that dozens of volunteers in communities across B.C. and Canada are also serving heroically during any flood season. We are thankful for them.

I'll be thinking about this when I pass that point on Hwy 3.

THE BIG FALL

Canada Day celebrations featured some spectacular skydiving. I think I'd be very reluctant to try it, especially when I consider the following story. In 1999 Joan Murray of Charlotte, N.C. skydived from an altitude of 14,500 feet. Her parachute did not open. Desperate attempts finally deployed the reserve chute at 700 feet but it very quickly failed as well. She hit the ground at 80 mph but fortunately on a somewhat soft anthill. Unfortunately it was inhabited by a massive colony of fire ants. Doctors surmised that the more than 200 bites may have sent such a shock through her shattered body that it kept her heart beating and may have been a factor in sparing her life. Two years later she strapped on an undoubtedly double-checked parachute for her 37th skydive.

Source: Publications International, 2012 p. 650 Louis Weber COO

What does it take to make me want to quit? How much determination and perseverance does it take to keep going? While we may consider Joan Murray's decision a foolish one she may well have advice for the rest of us. Was it W. Churchill who advised us to "Never, never, never give up?" There are things we should be giving up, and some things we shouldn't even try, but others require perseverance. By the way, throughout life God doesn't give up on us!

See you at the finish line.

SPELUNKERS

A spelunker is one who makes a hobby out of exploring and studying caves. Exploring caves is an enticing adventure. I am not a spelunker but have visited caves with stalagmites and stalactites, huge caverns and side passages, underground lakes and marvelous formations. I've experienced the utter blackness of lights out. It can be exciting but only if you are sure of the way out. News coverage of a coach and 12 teens from a soccer team lost in a cave system in Thailand illustrates that. What a frightening experience it must have been to be trapped in a place like that. Black darkness, hunger, thirst, despair, thoughts of impending death and who knows what else, must have been terrifying. What a huge relief to know that they were found even though rescue is still a very difficult task.

Consider the world's largest cave system. Early guide Stephen Bishop called these caves a "grand, gloomy and peculiar place". Its vast chambers and complex labyrinths have earned its name - Mammoth.

Since the 1972 unification of Mammoth Cave with the even-longer system under Flint Ridge to the north, the official name of the system has been the Mammoth-Flint Ridge Cave System of south central Kentucky. This is the world's longest known cave system, with more than 400 miles explored so far. It is nearly twice as long as the second-longest cave system, Mexico's Sac Actun underwater cave.

What would it feel like to be lost in a system like that? Undoubtedly some people feel as though their whole life is that way. They feel imprisoned by circumstances, dysfunctional relationships, overpowering addictions and lack of meaning or significance in life. This is not the way life is supposed to be. After being found, that coach and those 12 teens would certainly not declare, "We knew the way out. We didn't need help." We also need a saviour and a guide. Was it Augustine who concluded that we all have a huge 'hole' in our life that only God can fill? People try to stuff it full with fun and games (pleasure), money and things (possessions), influence and control (power) and/or recognition and achievement (prestige). We all need a measure of each one of these but if even one of them is the priority in life we have enthroned a false god. Jesus stated, "I am the way." He didn't just claim to know the way to an abundant life, He said, "I am the Way"! I realize that many would think of Him as a fairy-tale legend, a deranged lunatic or an outright liar, but I believe He is exactly what He claimed. He is the Lord! He can rescue us out of the dark cave and into amazing light!

It's bright ahead on the sunny side.

THERAPY FOR OUR SPIRITUAL MUSCLES

Some time ago I sought the help of a massage therapist for relief from muscle pain that had plagued me for weeks. In the series of treatments I recognized some comparison and some contrasts between the treatment process and the way God seeks to bring about therapy for our spiritual muscles.

1. Massage therapy starts when I ask for it. God works in our lives to bring us to the point of asking for His help. *"Whosoever shall call upon the name of the Lord shall be saved." Romans 10:13* But we need to be humble enough to ask for it. Then comes the process of Christian growth (spiritual muscles).

2. The process usually brings on some pain before I gain recovery. This also applies when God decides to work on my spiritual muscles.

3. I was repeatedly advised to let go, not resist, and not tense up in order for the therapist to be effective. God also calls on me to let go of stubborn ways and allow Him to direct and correct.

4. Refusing to cooperate just makes matters worse.

5. Last, it isn't enough to just go along with all this during the therapy session. There are exercises and lifestyle habits that I must incorporate. Unless I consistently put into practice what God is teaching me I will also not gain strength for my spiritual muscles.

"Be strong in the Lord and in the power of His might." Ephesians 6:10

TODDLER IN THE WELL

Chantal Porter glanced out the window of her Del Rey Oaks, Calif. home to check on her two young children in the back yard. It was a warm, mid-December morning, 1980. She spotted four year old Quincyann but not 15 month old Christopher. A deeply concerned search brought no results. Then she spotted the nine to ten inch well hole her husband had been digging with an auger. Surely he could not have slipped down there. The shaft of the auger protruded from the hole and the unmistakable crying confirmed the worst.

Panic stricken, she summoned police, firemen and ambulance. A light aimed down the shaft showed he had slid down feet first and was wedged in just above the auger. A hose was lowered to provide air but attempts to pull up the auger would severely injure or even kill the boy. Additionally it could dislodge dirt and suffocate the lad. The only solution was to dig a large, deep hole nearby, gently, and then tunnel horizontally to the boy. The top backhoe operator, Harold Clark, was enlisted for this very delicate maneuver. Too much vibration would cause the shaft to cave in and suffocate the lad. 45 minutes later he had a 22 foot hole. Another two hours of three men digging the tunnel by hand, shored up by boiler plates they brought in, reached the lad. It could have easily been a disastrous result instead.

Parents, Jeff and Chantal, plus others from their church prayed fervently throughout the ordeal. At about six pm one of the men brought the slightly injured boy to his grateful parents. Their response was "Thank you, Jesus" and thank you to all the rescuers and those who helped support the family.

Amazing rescue.

TOWER ONE RESCUE

Stanley Praimnath was a banker working on the 81st floor of Tower One. On the morning of Sept.11, 2001 he had felt a need to pray earnestly for his own safety and the welfare of his family. He didn't know why but he spent extra time asking the Lord to protect him that day. To quote him, *"For some particular reason I gave the Lord a little extra of myself that morning. I said, Lord, cover me and all my loved ones under your precious blood. And even though I said that and believed it, I said it over and over and over."*

Glancing out the window at work, he noticed that Tower Two was on fire. He and a friend decided to evacuate but a security guard assured him that Tower One was safe. Back in his office a second look out the window revealed that an American Airlines plane was headed straight for him. He frantically ducked under the desk and curled up in a fetal position shortly before it hit only 20 feet away from him. The wing of the plane was ablaze in the doorway to the offices. He was also trapped by rubble and could not move. He prayed for help and suddenly felt like *"the strongest man alive"*. He escaped from the debris, dodged the flames but found all exits blocked and he trapped against a wall. He made contact with a man on the other side of the wall. Together they broke a hole through it and found a stairway. On the concourse at the bottom flames confronted them. Dousing themselves under the sprinklers they fled through the flames to safety.

I don't know all the answers to why some are rescued and others not. I don't know why I was born in a relatively peaceful and prosperous country while others suffer war, famine and poverty. But we can all be thankful for what we do have.

Grateful for the sunny side.

TRUST ME

An orchardist was going through some deep and troubling difficulties. They were testing him to the point where even his trust in God's care for him was wavering. Nothing seemed to be going right. The problems were more than he could handle. In an attempt to clear his mind and think through his problems he resorted to a walk in the orchard that meant so much to him. His five year-old son had followed him, unaware of the distress his father was in. They came to an old apple tree destined to be cut down. It had outlived its profitability. "Just like me," the orchardist mused. "Maybe I'm no good anymore either."

"Daddy, daddy! Can I climb that old apple tree?" pleaded his son. The father sensed the benefit of a diversion so he stood underneath as the boy climbed, but some of the branches showed signs of weakness. The boy had ventured out on a limb that threatened to break. There was a danger that he would come crashing down. "Jump, Buddy," shouted the father, "I'll catch you!" "Shall I let go of everything and trust you?" asked the lad. "Yes," replied the father. The boy let go and landed safely in the father's arms. Then the implication hit the orchardist. If I want my son to let go and trust me when he's in trouble, shouldn't I be willing to let go and trust my Father for things I can't handle?

"Cast all your care upon Him for He cares for you." 1 Peter 5:7

The father's perspective changed. The problems hadn't gone away but the things that really mattered – his relationship to his family and to God – weren't gone either. He returned to the house encouraged.

THEME 15

Sin

Am I really such a bad sinner?

"… all have sinned and fall short of the glory of God."
Romans 3:23

TO BE, OR NOT TO BE, ANGRY

Have you ever felt a surge of anger rise up within you when some driver cuts you off or darts between your car and the one in front of you, forcing you to slam on your brakes? Have you ever wanted to give others a piece of your mind for the way they treated you? Have there been times when life has been so difficult and empty that you feel like lashing out at whoever comes by?

We have seen the violent results of such anger on the newscasts, in the schools, in our communities and maybe even in our family. We usually become angry when we are not appreciated, when we are hurt in some way, when others are honored ahead of us or if someone gets something we wanted. In these cases anger is likely to make things worse instead of better. They are based on self-centeredness. They are motivated by a "me first" mindset.

There is a place for anger when a good cause is at stake. Anger can become channeled energy for correcting wrongs. Ephesians 4:26 says, *"In your anger do not sin. Do not let the sun go down on your anger."* The only time it's not a sin to get angry is when you get angry at sin.

But how can we ever become like that? It's only when we experience the grace of God in forgiving us, instead of condemning us, that we can also extend grace to others.

Ephesians 2:7-9 tells us about *"the incomparable riches of his grace, expressed in his kindness to us in Christ Jesus. For it is by grace you have been saved, through faith -- and this not from yourselves, it is the gift of God -- not by works, so that no one can boast."*

May it be that you have experienced the grace of God.

MAKING ASSUMPTIONS

Even though the gauge told me we were low on gasoline I drove past the filling station and aimed for one I knew was some distance up ahead. I assumed it would be open but it wasn't. The consequence was obvious but not nearly as severe as the airplane that took off after refueling on the assumption that the attendant had done it correctly. As it turned out the number of **gallons** requested was given in **liters**, resulting in only about a quarter of what was needed. Many of us remember the amazingly spectacular emergency landing that the pilot accomplished at Gimley, MB without power. The consequences could have been death for all but no one died.

One of the more horrible accounts of bad assumptions relates to a couple leaving their infant in the care of a baby-sitter while on holidays. In itself that is fine but when the baby-sitter seemed to be a little late, they became impatient and decided to go, leaving the door unlocked on the assumption that the sitter would arrive soon. When the sitter came and gained no response to her knock on the door she assumed the people had changed their minds and went back home. The infant starved to death in the highchair. The consequences were severe.

In the seventh chapter of the Gospel of John Jesus was being confronted by the crowds and the religious leaders. A controversy arose among them as to whether He might be the Messiah. One group based its conclusion on the fact that He came from Galilee and could not be the Messiah because that person was to be born in Bethlehem. They rejected Him on a false assumption. That had serious consequences.

There are many opinions circulating amongst us today about who Jesus really is. Is He just a myth, a legend? Was He a lunatic or a liar? Or was He really the Son of God coming with an amazing offer? The offer was: let me take the blame for your sin and I'll give you my righteousness; let me pay your debt and you can have my bank account. Check it out. Don't reject the offer on an assumption that there is nothing to it.

BREXIT??

This recently much-used term could spawn a few additions to our vocabulary. It may be that others have suggested similar words, but here are my suggestions.

Chexit – a cheque that bounces for lack of funds

Flexit – a guy who tries to display muscles he hasn't got

Hexit – malicious plans that didn't work out

Nexit – an attempted embrace that earns a slap in the face

Wrexit – and unlicensed teen who 'borrows' dad's car

E-jexit – pushing the delete button on an unwanted email

There's a place for a bit of humor to send a ray of light into the gloom of some bad days.

How about **rejexit** for the person who benefits from all the good things that God has created (food, air, water, an amazingly complex body, a very dependable set of nature's laws, etc.) without being grateful? Then that person wants appreciation for what they do and justice when he/she is mistreated. The amazing part is that God keeps on loving us all anyway.

CHAINS

During the Prussian War a French blacksmith was taken prisoner by the German army. "Do not worry about me," he secretly reported to his family. "When I am bound I shall carefully study the chains that fetter me until I discover the weakest link. Then, when no one is looking, I shall break the chain and go free."

According to plan, when the opportunity came, he studied the links, but soon sank back in hopeless despair. He saw that he was bound with chains that he himself had made. His captors had taken them from his shop. There were no weak links.

The blacksmith is to be commended for making strong chains. However, bad habits can be like very strong chains that bind us. The habits may start weakly and almost innocently but eventually become unintentionally just as hard to break as real chains. By contrast, good habits have to be cultivated in a disciplined and intentional way to become strong. That makes life challenging.

THOSE PESKY DANDELIONS

Those pesky dandelions! I thought I was finished with them after the spring onslaught but here were a few more poking their heads up through the lawn grass. The lawn had looked so green and pure and now this. They are just like sin that keeps coming back at us.

One response could be, "Why bother?" After all they are flowers so just let them be. Go with a dandelion lawn. What does it matter? Postmodern philosophy thinks that way about sin. Moral principles are just social constructions that we devise artificially. We can create our own truth. There are no absolutes. Go with whatever suits you. That may be OK for dandelions but not for what's wrong with our world.

We usually don't accept dandelions that way and we certainly can't deal with sin that way either. Sin is not a fabrication. It's for real with real consequences. You have to get it out with the roots, keep on top of it and not let it get the upper hand. Thankfully the Lord offers us a solution. He is able to cleanse us from them, take the penalty for us and also provide the power over sin we need in daily life.

"Come now, let us reason together," says the Lord. "Though your sins are like scarlet they shall be white as snow; though they are red as crimson, they shall be like wool." Isaiah 1:18

MASTER DETECTIVES

We may be thrilled when crime scene investigators solve a case by detecting small but conclusive evidence. That is remarkable. Very minute detection can occur using nature's electromagnetic spectrum (EMS).

The EMS spans a huge range of wave lengths: from 300m AM radio waves, to short waves, TV & FM radio, cellular, microwaves, radar, WiFi, millimeter waves, telemetry, infrared, visible light, ultraviolet, X-rays and finally to the extremely minute, atom-sized gamma rays. Notice that visible light waves that allow us to see fall between the infrared and ultraviolet range. That's only a small part of the EM spectrum. There's a whole lot going on that we can't see. For details use a computer to search for the electromagnetic spectrum chart.

If a scientist can measure the wavelength emitted with a spectrometer he/she knows <u>what material</u> is present because elemental materials give off a specific wave length. Then, if a scientist can also measure how intensely a certain wave length is reflected by a solute in a solution, she/he knows <u>how much</u> of it is there. A spectrophotometer does that, even if there is only a minute amount present. These instruments already existed in the 1960s. Now they are even more advanced.

This ability is put to use in detecting the level of pollutants in the air. It can also measure tiny amounts of poison in the blood. Since we can use the laws of nature for such exact detection it is no stretch to believe that God can detect and record all our words, deeds and even our thoughts. *Psalm 139:2, 4 "...you perceive my thoughts from afar."* *"Before a word is on my tongue you know it completely."*

We can't get away with anything, but by the grace of God the sacrifice of Jesus paid for the cost of wiping away everything for those who trust Him with that.

Hallelujah!

FRAUDS AND SCAMS

I dropped what I was doing to answer the telephone, only to hear someone claiming that "my computer was in serious trouble and on the verge of a crash. We can help you." Many of you will have had similar fraudulent calls: threats of arrest due to delinquent income taxes, fake prizes, unbelievable inheritances, or false pleas for donations to charities. It's enough to make a person irate.

Then a thought struck me. Anger will get me nowhere, I need a positive counter-offensive move. So, during several of the next calls the conversation went approximately as follows.

Caller: "We are getting error messages from your computer and as an authorized partner of Microsoft we are calling to solve the problem."

Me: "Which computer is in difficulty? I have a desktop, a laptop and another older one."

Caller: "The one on Windows."

I explain that each one is on a different Windows operating system. If they are going to fix it they must know which Windows program it is. If they say it is the older one, I tell them it has been in my closet for months, disconnected from the internet and not even plugged into power. If they hesitate to choose one computer I respond about as follows.

Me: "Did you know that a record is being kept of all the words, actions and even thoughts of yours right now? Did you know that Someone knows exactly what you are doing?"

Caller: "That is impossible."

Me: "No, it isn't. God has had a super, super 'computer' since time began. It is light years ahead of the best we've got. Listen to Psalm 139:1-4. *"O Lord, you have searched me and you know me. You know when I sit and when I rise; you perceive my thoughts from afar. You discern my going out and my lying down; you are familiar with all my ways. Before a word is on my tongue you know it completely, O Lord."*

Caller: "I don't believe it."

Me: "There is a Judgment Day coming and unless you find a way to wipe all that off the record you will be held accountable for it. But there is good news!" *(Click! He hung up on me before I could tell him the good news!)* He could have learned that Someone is offering to pay the penalty for him. It cost Jesus his life on the cross. If he were willing to acknowledge God as the one he is accountable to, admit his sin and ask forgiveness, God would give it freely. After that He'd also help him to live right. This is no scam or fraud.

We've had very few calls since then. I almost miss getting them.

GARBAGE

I took out the garbage, a weekly routine. Then I began to think about how important this unpleasant weekly task is. What would it be like if we couldn't get rid of garbage? Come to think of it, our bodies have the most efficient and unique garbage disposal system on the planet. The same red corpuscles that deliver oxygen to the lungs pick up the carbon dioxide and perhaps other waste. We wouldn't want our groceries delivered by the garbage truck!! Both the carbon dioxide and perhaps certain wastes pass through membranes into the lung's 300,000 air sacs without losing any blood.

Our kidneys filter out liquid, toxic wastes while the intestines that have gleaned nutrients eventually excrete unwanted solid wastes. We'd be dead in a very short time if even one of these functions failed. It's a complex, created design, not the product of chance. Our life depends on it. We've got to regularly dispose of garbage.

Are we getting rid of toxins in our social, spiritual and emotional life? Bluntly speaking are we letting resentments, bitterness, hatred, anger, pride and numerous other 'garbage' pile up inside? It is very hard to consistently rid ourselves of these sins, but it is such a relief to know that our Savior can completely cleanse us from all sin. Check out 1 John 1:9.

THE GREAT NON-ESCAPE

Monday morning, after Sunday's rain, I was out on a walk and noticed that the roadway had many earthworms on it. The worms had sought refuge from the waterlogged lawns and grassy areas. It must have been a feeling of relief when they found a drier place. What they did not know was that the rain would stop and the sun was about to rise. What at first must have felt warm and comfortable soon became blistering heat. They could not dig down through the concrete and did not succeed in returning to the place they came from. Except for the ones I threw back onto the grass, they died a horrible death.

What are the deceitful escapes we might resort to when circumstances overwhelm us? People commit themselves to one or more of the following four things in an effort to find the security and fulfillment they seek.

1. Pleasure – everything has to be fun. The mindset is to deny ourselves no indulgence. The ultimate expression of this is promiscuous immorality and damaging addictions. The result is just the opposite of what was hoped for.
2. Possessions – get rich. Where the dollar is the paramount motivator we see many examples of huge disappointments and ruined relationships.
3. Prestige – get famous, achieve greatness. If our goal is to gain honor for ourselves the emptiness of life will soon overtake us.
4. Power – be in charge, have influence. We've watched multiple examples of cruel dictatorships that result from extreme pursuit of power.

All four of the above are valid secondary components in life. It is just that none of them will be fulfilling if it is number one in priority. The Scriptures make it very clear as to what needs to be number one.

Mark 12:30-31 "Love the Lord your God with all your heart and with all your soul and with all your mind and with all your strength. The second is this: Love your neighbor as yourself. There is no commandment greater than these."

The four pursuits mentioned above are in place if they are used to support our relationship with God and others but are fruitless escapes if they are the lone goal.

Keep on the sunny side but stay out of the blistering heat.

I AM METH

This poem was written by a young girl who was in jail for drug charges and was addicted to meth. She wrote this while in jail. As you will soon read, she fully grasped the horrors of the drug, as she tells in this simple,

Henry G Wiebe

yet profound poem. She was released from jail, but, true to her story, the drug owned her. They found her dead not long after, with the needle still in her arm. This thing is worse than any of us realize.

I destroy homes, I tear families apart, I take your children, and that's just the start.
I'm more costly than diamonds, more precious than gold, The sorrow I bring is a sight to behold.

If you need me, remember I'm easily found, I live all around you - in schools and in town.
I live with the rich, I live with the poor, I live down the street, and maybe next door.

I'm made in a lab, but not like you think, I can be made under the kitchen sink,
in your child's closet, and even in the woods, if this scares you to death, well it certainly should.

I have many names, but there's one you know best, I'm sure you've heard of me, my name is crystal meth.
My power is awesome, try me, you'll see. But if you do, you may never break free.

Just try me once and I might let you go, but try me twice, and I'll own your soul.
When I possess you, you'll steal and you'll lie. You do what you have to -- just to get high.

The crimes you'll commit for my narcotic charms will be worth the pleasure you'll feel in your arms.
You'll lie to your mother, you'll steal from your dad. When you see their tears, you should feel sad.
But you'll forget your morals and how you were raised. I'll be your conscience, I'll teach you my ways.

234

I take kids from parents, and parents from kids. I turn people
from God, and separate friends.
I'll take everything from you, your looks and your pride, I'll
be with you always -- right by your side.

You'll give up everything - your family, your home, your
friends, your money, then you'll be alone.
I'll take and take, till you have nothing more to give. When
I'm finished with you, you'll be lucky to live.

If you try me be warned - this is no game. If given the chance,
I'll drive you insane.
I'll ravish your body, I'll control your mind. I'll own you
completely, your soul will be mine.
The nightmares I'll give you while lying in bed, the voices
you'll hear, from inside your head.
The sweats, the shakes, the visions you'll see, I want you to
know, these are all gifts from me.
But then it's too late, and you'll know in your heart, that you
are mine, and we shall not part.
You'll regret that you tried me, they always do, but you came
to me, not I to you.

You knew this would happen, many times you were told, but
you challenged my power, and chose to be bold.
You could have said no, and just walked away. If you could
live that day over, now what would you say?

I'll be your master, you will be my slave, I'll even go with you,
when you go to your grave.
Now that you have met me, what will you do? Will you try
me or not? It's all up to you.
I can bring you more misery than words can tell, Come take
my hand, let me lead you to hell.

Henry G Wiebe

THE PARADOX OF OUR TIME

In 1995, Dr. Bob Moorehead, pastor of Overlake Christian Church, in WA., USA, published a collection of his writings called *Words Aptly Spoken*. A small part of it is the following apt description that still mirrors the times we are in. BUT, it doesn't have to be like that for us individually. We can be different in our sphere of influence.

> *The paradox of our time in history is that we have taller buildings, but shorter tempers; wider freeways, but narrower viewpoints. We spend more, but have less; we buy more, but enjoy it less. We have bigger houses and smaller families; more conveniences, but less time. We have more degrees, but less sense; more knowledge, but less judgment; more experts, but more problems; more medicine, but less wellness.*
>
> *We drink too much, smoke too much, spend too recklessly, laugh too little, drive too fast, get too angry too quickly, stay up too late, get up too tired, read too seldom, watch TV too much, and pray too seldom. We have multiplied our possessions, but reduced our values. We talk too much, love too seldom, and hate too often. We've learned how to make a living, but not a life; we've added years to life, not life to years.*
>
> *We've been all the way to the moon and back, but have trouble crossing the street to meet the new neighbor. We've conquered outer space, but not inner space. We've done larger things, but not better things. We've cleaned up the air, but polluted the soul. We've split the atom, but not our prejudice. We write more, but learn less. We plan more, but accomplish less. We've learned to rush, but not to wait. We build more computers to hold more information to produce more copies than ever, but have less communication.*

Perhaps depressing, but he was right about much of it. Let's be among those who are not like that.

PUFFED UP

A gardener came across a small snake amongst the vegetable plants. It looked lifeless, but when he nudged it with a stick it reacted in a surprising way. The snake began to increase in size. Its head and body swelled up and the snake hissed in anger. It was a puff adder. Some puff adders in Africa are poisonous but in America they are usually harmless. There is a small fish in southern waters that will react in a similar way when caught and hauled out of the water. Undoubtedly it is a defense mechanism given to the adder and the fish by the Creator.

We human beings have a puffed up defense mechanism of our own. We pretend to be something we are not. Usually it means we pretend to be better at something than is true of us. Often others can see through that but occasionally we manage to fool them. That is not the case with God. He can easily tell what we are really like inside. Psalm 139 declares that He has searched us and knows us through and through. Fortunately for us He is also gracious and forgiving to those who will acknowledge sin and seek cleansing.

That will put us on the sunny side.

SPLINTERS

I was walking on the bedroom carpet in my bare feet when a wooden splinter poked painfully into the bottom of my foot. How did that get there? I immediately pulled away at the splinter but the tip broke off and stayed under the skin. Repeated efforts with a pair of tweezers merely exacerbated the situation. I figured I should just leave it. It's small. I thought I had dug most of it out. It'll just go away. By the third day I became painfully aware that all was not well. A battle royal was in progress inside the wound between my immune system and the infection, with inflammation the evidence. Walking became very unpleasant. I soaked it in hot water and Epsom salt, applied some pressure to the base of the wound and out slid a half-inch splinter tip. There was significant immediate relief and much quicker healing.

It made me realize that life relationships are that way too. Leaving imbedded irritations, resentments, anger and the like inadequately dealt with will cause festering and pain. Little problems become big ones. Relationships suffer. The joy of life drains away. It may take some pressure to have it out in the open and resolved but that is worth it.

Don't let little irritations fester into big problems.

PLUGGED SPRINKLERS & BROKEN PIPES

Underground irrigation systems have also been called 'automatic' irrigation. I've come to the conclusion that, in some ways, they are not automatic at all. They need constant maintenance. Algae, dirt and even spider webs get into the system and plug up the holes in the sprinkler heads. Pipes get brittle over time, and break. I may step onto a sprinkler head or run the lawn mower too close when the 'pop-up' didn't pop down. I keep trying to get the best adjustment for the best coverage and haven't yet achieved it. The result is that I've made so many trips to the irrigation supply shop that I'm afraid they'll be designating a parking spot for me.

Wouldn't it be nice if the irrigation system were so automatic that it would repair itself, send cleaning agents when a sprinkler was blocked and constantly inject something that would keep the inside of the pipes clean? Come to think of it, our bodies have a system like that. Our circulatory system dispenses white blood cells and platelets to repair and clean our arteries and veins when cuts or infections occur. In addition, the red blood corpuscles deliver nutrients and pick up garbage from the cells. Amazing provision by an amazing Creator. When the damage to our circulation system is too severe He has given us brains to devise medical solutions for at least some of them.

However, life doesn't automatically run that smoothly or correct itself. We constantly need to be cleaning up our act, repairing relationships or making adjustments to our plans because there are right and wrong ways to do things. It's humbling and frustrating business but the result can be even more beautiful than a well-watered lawn and garden or a clean blood circulation system. Isaiah 1:18 gives us great hope, *"Though your sins be as scarlet they shall be white as snow."*

TAX COLLECTOR

He was in turmoil inside. The agony and guilt of his lifestyle were plaguing him severely. Former friends shunned him. His family was ostracized. The riches he had accumulated were ill-gotten gains that didn't bring him the happiness he had hoped for. The leaders of his community considered him a traitor because he worked for the hated Roman conquerors. He collected taxes for the Romans and charged extra for his own benefit. He thought it would make his life comfortable. The result was anything but comfortable. Most of all he felt completely estranged from God.

What should he do now? In his desperation he found his way to the temple in Jerusalem. To his chagrin he spotted a Pharisee, a so-called holy man, nearby. The tax collector hesitated but his need was so great that he ignored what would undoubtedly be the accusing looks of the self-righteous Pharisee who would likely be thinking that this guy doesn't deserve to be here. He should be kicked out.

The tax collector could hear the Pharisee's proud prayer. *"God, I thank you that I am not like other men – robbers, evildoers, adulterers -or even like this tax collector. I fast twice a week and give a tenth of all I get."* Luke 18:11 He thought God was lucky to have him around.

"He's right," the tax collector must have thought. *"I don't deserve mercy from God. I can't pray like he does."* In his despair he could only manage one sentence, *"God have mercy on me, a sinner."* In that one sentence the tax collector did the three things that counted. He acknowledged God as the Lord he was accountable to, he admitted he was a sinner and he asked for mercy. It was granted. Jesus' comment was, *"I tell you that this man, rather than the other, went home justified before God. For everyone who exalts himself will be humbled, and he who humbles himself will be exalted."* See Luke 18:9-14

I've used some imagination for the build-up to the temple scene but it is likely close to what went on. The main idea is biblical. The triple A plan is still what God expects from us: acknowledge, admit, ask.

THEAGENES: OLYMPIC WRESTLER

Theagenes was famous in Greek history for his prowess as a wrestler. It is reputed that at age nine he spotted the statue of a god in the marketplace in Thasos that somehow challenged him to wrestle it off its moorings. He broke it off and carried it home. Later his punishment consisted of only carrying it back.

As an adult Theagenes won the wrestling crown in the early Olympics. No competitor was ever able to defeat him. This deeply affected one of his opponents. After Theagenes' death this continuously envious opponent was constantly irritated to see Theagenes' statue in the town where he had broken off a statue at age nine. Maybe he could defeat him symbolically now. In his rage the competitor attacked the statue of Theagenes, wrestling it off the base. In the process the statue toppled and fell onto the envious opponent, killing him.

We don't know how accurate this account is but we do know that envy and jealousy will hurt us more than the person we envy. Rare is the athlete in our current Olympics who can genuinely congratulate someone who defeated him or her. Just as rare is the person in daily life who actually can give credit to someone who is doing a better job. We each have an ability in which we shine, and we each need to honor the abilities of others where they shine.

The right attitude will help to keep things sunny.

TRUTH?

It has been said that truth is like surgery, it hurts at the time but often helps to bring on the cure. Lies are like illicit drugs, they temporarily make a person feel better but afterwards have serious side effects.

Lies range from intentionally cruel deceit to seemingly trivial half-truths. One area where many of us may unintentionally encroach on telling lies is when we make exaggerated statements like the following ones.

> *You never are there for me when I need you.*
> *You are always going out shopping or having coffee somewhere.*
> *Nobody does it that way.*
> *Everybody gets to go except me. (Add your own examples.)*

The same general idea applies to the opposite approach, flattery.

Right now someone may be thinking that it surely would be good if a certain couple read this. Hold on a bit. Maybe they are sending you a copy.

On the brighter side, when we are careful about what we say and how we say it, people are much more likely to listen and to appreciate what we declare. This will generate pleasant relationships instead of conflicts. Let's say what we mean and mean what we say, but do it calmly and respectfully. That is really tough to do but very necessary.

WORDS

The air was filled with threats and curses. The neighbor was so angry with what the person next door had done that he lost his temper totally. It almost descended into violence. A few days later when things had quietened down somewhat he was confronted by a small group of people for the way he had acted. He denied it all. "I didn't say that!" "I didn't swear at him." "I was simply explaining to him that what he had done wasn't right."

The neighbor's son, whose bedroom window faced the scene of the conflict, had made a recording of the interaction. He produced it and began to play it. At this the one who had denied it was faced with the evidence. He hurriedly left the group, ostensibly to fulfill an 'errand'.

This not-so-imaginary event reminded me of the statement in Matthew 12:36 *"...men will have to give account on the day of judgment for every careless word they have spoken."* I need to keep my words soft and respectful; I never know when I might have to 'eat' them. Although I, and perhaps all of you, have not been guilty of an act like the illustration above, I know that if all my unkind words, deeds and thoughts were posted on the walls of my house they would cover the inside and outside. Gratefully, Jesus has offered to pay the penalty for everything we ever did, said or even thought. It cost Him His life blood. Wow! That is grace!

How could we refuse an offer like that?

THEME 16

Suffering

Why do good people suffer bad things?

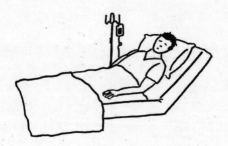

"The apostles left the Sanhedrin, rejoicing because they had been counted worthy of suffering disgrace for the Name." Acts 5:41

ADVERSITY

All of us have to contend with adversity repeatedly. Whenever our goal is blocked, we don't get what we wanted or someone/something fights against us, we experience adversity. It's really difficult to revel in the biblical advice to count it all joy when we encounter adversity. How could that possibly be the right response?

At a time like that we need to remember that God is interested in our comfort and growth as a person but not at the expense of character. His goal for us may well require Him to deprive us of some pleasure, some possessions, or other pursuits because they are hindering the character development He really wants. The natural tendency for us is to tell God to stay out of our lives unless we ask for help. He is just not going to give in to that.

God is more concerned about my character than my comfort.

BURDENS

A medical missionary to Abyssinia, Dr. Lambie, learned a valuable lesson by observing a practice of the people native to the land. Not having many bridges over streams that at times were torrential, they adopted an unusual process for wading across safely. They would carry a sack full of stones as they crossed. Without that burden on their back their footing on the sometimes slippery creek bottom would be easily lost due to the force of the current. It's much like the practice of adding weight to the back of the pickup truck in snowy weather to gain traction.

We are inclined to complain about burdens we have to bear in life. They are such a pain. While many of them are a huge hindrance it may also be true that some of them are designed to keep our feet on the ground and give us traction. We often learn things in the tough times that good times would never teach us. If you are burdened down with discouragingly heavy and difficult situations, consider this illustration. There may be a sunny side to the situation.

CONTRARY WIND

While waiting for his son to arrive at the airport the father noticed a pilot standing nearby. Curious about the answer to a question that had puzzled him for some time, he approached the pilot and asked, "Why do planes take off against the wind? It would seem that they could gain more speed for take-off if they went with the wind."

Patiently the pilot explained that going into the wind actually helps by increasing the lift factor for take-off. In addition, tail winds are very dangerous because they hinder the ability to control flight. Contrary winds can be helpful.

Each one of us has likely often complained about things that are working against us. We don't realize that sometimes that very opposition sharpens our resolve and forces us to increase our fervour. Although that is not true of every contrary experience, some of them can give us needed teachable moments and stronger motivation.

'Contrary winds' can turn troubles into blessings.

DEW

Some time ago I walked out onto our lawn and noticed that a heavy dew had settled onto the grass. It had been a cool, still night in contrast to the hot, sunny day. Those are the conditions that cause evaporation during the day and condensation during the night. Coolness and relative calm in the air during the dark night after a hot day will bring down the dew.

It made me think of some cold, dark 'nights' I experienced in life. I didn't like those times, but just like plants that benefit from the dew I needed to be still and let the circumstances teach me something. We often learn the most from the dark and troubled times of life. Then we also appreciate the sunny times more.

LOONS

The surface of the lake was like a glass mirror. Not a ripple was to be seen anywhere. A loon emerged from a fishing foray under water and decided to leave the lake, perhaps to a better fishing spot. There was much flapping of wings and churning of the water as the loon tried to take off. The loon's body was just too heavy and the wings were unable to create enough lift. What was needed was a headwind to race into and create the lift as the air rushed over the wings. No amount of repeated, exhausting attempts without a breeze allowed the loon to take off. Eventually a wind did come and the loon successfully soared away.

Perhaps there are times when adversity provides the impetus for us to rise to the occasion. Maybe contrary winds are actually just what we needed in certain circumstances.

Turn adversity into a teacher instead of a destroyer.

GRATEFUL FOR PAIN

WHAT!! Thankful for pain? You've got to be kidding! Yes. We actually need to be thankful for pain! Pain is not an enemy, it is a gift. Right now some of you are thinking that I am nuts. Read on!!

Leprosy patients lose sensitivity to pain. Walking barefoot brings on cuts and bruises that are not noticed. Infection sets in with disastrous results. Rats chewing on fingers or ears while the person sleeps are not even noticed. Fingers and toes can be amputated without the patient feeling it. Boiling water spilled on you wouldn't hurt. There are no warning signals, no alarm bells ringing in the brain. The message doesn't reach the brain. This tells us that it is the brain that senses the problem and declares its existence by using pain. We need the warning message to avoid disastrous consequences.

We are aware that many people have severe, ongoing pain from a variety of causes. They don't need ongoing messages about pain. Nor does it help for them to be told to look on the bright side, it's a wonderful life. All of us probably know people in that condition. My wife was diagnosed with Parkinson's in 2005 and it is horrible and very frustrating for her. We feel for them. So what is the role of painkillers? If they are used without also dealing with the problem it is like turning off a smoke alarm and ignoring the advancing fire. If it alerts us to the problem and we deal with it, we don't need the message repeated. Then it is fitting to use a pain killer because the message has been heeded.

Physical pain is not the only kind that affects us. There is relational pain. Broken relationships may result in broken hearts or even ruined lives. Our conscience sends warning signals which, if ignored, will allow the relational problem to fester. On the positive side, this tells us how soothing, healing and uplifting good relationships are.

Our body is equipped to build up a resistance to some forms of pain. Guitar players develop callouses on fingertips and it no longer hurts. Feet develop hardened soles when used constantly barefooted. These are positive things. Relationally we can also become calloused to the pain inflicted on others by bullying, constant criticisms or even violent acts. In an extreme cases, serial killers and mass murderers lose the sense of guilt or compassion. These are very negative results. We need to heed relational pain.

Yes, we definitely need to be thankful for much of the pain that comes our way. It carries the message that there is a problem that needs fixing or the consequences can be huge, whether physical or relational.

But it is tough be thankful for the message pain is sending.

The Gift of Pain by Phillip Yancy and Dr.
Paul Brand, especially p.43 – 45.

PEARLS

When a parasite or some other irritating, foreign object gets inside the shell of certain mollusks, it doesn't have the ability to expel it. Instead it secretes a calcium carbonate based substance plus conchiolin to encase the intruder. Once the beginning of this layering is underway the mantle on the inside of the mollusk takes over. In time it coats the object with microscopic layers of crystals that produce a tapestry of refracted light and color. The number of layers determines the level of iridescence and thereby the value of the pearl.

What do we do with irritants that get under our skin, as it were? Physically our body's immune system sends phagocytes (our soldiers) to engulf the antigen (enemy irritant). When successful they prevent disease. When it comes to our relational life we often don't 'lovingly cover' the problem. We may lash out against someone, claw at the problem or generally attack someone in a way that makes things worse. A better way is to learn from the mollusk to use a plan that builds character. That will produce a gem.

It is worth noting that scientists have not yet succeeded in duplicating the process of producing a pearl of equivalent quality. That defense mechanism remains a prized secret. It is also worth noting that vinegar can dissolve a pearl. Perhaps this tells us how a sour attitude over an irritation can destroy what might have been a gem. Such a reaction to a problem is tough to accomplish but it is worth the challenge to respond with love. *"Love covers a multitude of sins"*, it says in 1 Peter 4:8. If you can do that, you are producing a pearl.

WHY ME, GOD?

Stunned and shocked Leola Harmon saw a huge trailer truck drift into her lane. The driver was slumped over the wheel. There was no chance to avoid a head on collision! She smashed into the windshield, slammed back against the steering wheel and then was hurled through the glass onto a snowbank in Anchorage, Alaska. Barely conscious and coming out of a daze, she heard a voice saying, "It's alive – I saw it move!" She was an "it", mutilated beyond recognition. Even in her shattered state, as an air force nurse at Elmendorf Hospital in Nov., 1968, she realized the implications of that statement.

At that hospital, staff stared in horror at the sight of their emaciated friend. They seemed paralyzed into inaction. Dr. J. Stallings burst into the room and took charge. *"I'll do the tracheotomy. Gary, you work on her legs. Ray, get a venocath into her – she'll need blood and fluids. Major, tell X-ray to stand by. Nurse, call the operating room to get ready for orthopedic, obstetrics, general surgery, plastics and dental work. Round up every specialist on the base."*

Leola was five months pregnant, the baby was stillborn. Her husband came in with grief and pain on his face but when he saw the 'frightening stranger' he left without a word or a touch. In less than two years they divorced. *"Give me two to five years to make you at least presentable,"* the doctor told her. *"God saved your life. Now it's up to us to make the most of it. If you have the guts, I have the time and the skills."*

She lost her baby, her husband, her wellbeing and even her identity in one fell swoop. The swollen, discolored, distorted, toothless mass of tissue that was left comprised only a third of her face. It took years of plastic surgery, dental work and grafts from other parts of her body to rebuild. There were thirty-five operations in seven years, including four innovative surgeries created by the doctor. Even after she was released from the hospital, two Girl Scouts selling cookies were so frightened when she answered the door that they dropped the cookies and fled.

Eventually returning to work she became that doctor's research assistant and emergency nurse. Patients identified with her. When Dr. Stallings was gone for two months on an exchange appointment prior to setting up his own practice in Des Moines, Leola missed him terribly. His absence during those two months made her realize how dependent she had become on him. He wanted her to come with him as his nurse. But she decided it would not look good for a single nurse to follow a single doctor to Des Moines. She resolved to tell him when he returned that she would not be able to come. He responded by admitting to her that she was right and that he had missed her too. In a fumbling manner the doctor who was so in charge and so confident in his abilities had to muster the courage to say, "*I think we should get married before we go there.*" Leola became the wife of Dr. James O. Stallings and thanked God for giving her the answer to "Why Me?"

The road to recovery or success often leads through tough times.

Baes on Leola Harmon's own account in the Oct., 1976 Reader's Digest

THEME 17

Trust

Can the teachings of the Bible be trusted?

"Sanctify them by the truth; your word is truth." John 17:17

THE ANVIL

Last eve I passed beside a blacksmith's door,
And heard the anvil ring the vesper chime;
Then, looking in, I saw upon the floor
Old hammers, worn with beating years of time.

How many anvils have you had," said I,
"To wear and batter all these hammers so?"
"Just one," said he, and then, with twinkling eye,
"The anvil wears the hammers out, you know."

And so, thought I, the anvil of God's Word,
For ages skeptic blows have beat upon;
Yet, though the noise of falling blows was heard,
The anvil is unharmed--the hammers gone.

John Clifford

APPLE OF MY EYE

The expression used in the title was originally a reference to the value of the pupil of our eye. It is the most sensitive part. It contains the transparent, aqueous humor through which light enters that carries the image being seen. Therefore it is very precious. The promise "*I will guard you as the apple of my eye*" (Psalm 17:8) emphasizes that we would do whatever we can to prevent damage to that part in order not to lose our eyesight. When the Lord declared that whoever touches my people touches the apple of my eye He was making it very plain that he values His people a lot.

It may be difficult for some people to think that Almighty God would ever care enough about them to guard them that closely. We probably don't have the faintest idea of how often He has had to do that. As soon as something unpleasant happens to us we tend to think that God doesn't care. We dismiss the idea that there might be a good reason for that unpleasant event or circumstance. A measure of how much He does care would be *"God commends His love toward us in that while we were yet sinners, Christ died for us."* (Romans 5:8) What more evidence do we need that He cares when He was willing to die for us as payment for our iniquities?

You are loved.

BE STILL

A serious operation had put Marvin DeHaan into the Rochester, MN hospital for a fairly long recovery period. Used to being very active and busy he found the experience of being 'set aside' a bit of an ordeal. A friend sent him the following poem, author unknown.

> *I needed the quiet so he drew me aside*
> *Into the shadows where we could confide;*
> *Away from the bustle where all the day long*
> *I hurried and worried when active and strong.*
> *I needed the quiet though at first I rebelled,*
> *But gently – so gently my cross he upheld.*
> *And whispered so sweetly of spiritual things.*
> *Though weakened in body my spirit took wings*
> *To heights never dreamed of when active and gay;*
> *He loved me so greatly He drew me away.*
> *I needed the quiet, no prison my bed*
> *But a beautiful valley of blessing instead;*
> *A place to grow richer in Jesus to hide,*
> *I needed the quiet so he drew me aside.*

Being very busy isn't always the best.

FACES

A lot can be read from the look on a person's face. Even children can discern when it is a favorable time to make that special request. Often it is really hard to hide your true feelings from others who can see your face.

A German sculptor, Danniker, spent eight years trying to get just the right expression on a model of what he thought Jesus must have looked like. Some observers were overcome with emotion when they saw the result. He was then asked to do the same with the Greek goddess, Venus. He replied, "After gazing so long into the face of Christ, think you that I can now turn my attention to a heathen goddess?"

An infidel artist was commissioned to produce a caricature of a Salvation Army meeting in Sheffield, England. After scanning their faces that showed joy and peace he was convicted about his own sinfulness. He decided that he needed what they had.

The hymn writer, H. H. Lemmel, put it this way.

> *Turn your eyes upon Jesus, look full in His wonderful face;*
> *And the things of earth will grow strangely dim in the light of His*
> *glory and grace.*

That is a real sunny side.

HELP!!

Psalm 121 may well contain the reflections of a pilgrim on his trek to Jerusalem. While walking along difficult terrain his natural concern would have been about his safety as he walked. Danger from bandits was even more unsettling. His assurance was that his help came from the One who was powerful enough to create heaven and earth.

The pilgrim was in good hands in three ways and we can have the same help.

Sure footing underneath

"He will not let your foot slip" The trail could well be rocky. An injury from a fall while on the way would be disastrous. Our spiritual foundation also needs to be free of pitfalls. If moral principles and just practices crumble we are not on solid ground.

Protective shade above

The sun can be devastating on a long, hot, dusty trek. Both the sun and the moon are usually a welcome presence but the sun can deliver harmful rays. Our head is particularly vulnerable. In a spiritual sense we are also vulnerable to influences on our mind that are harmful. The Lord can provide the filter we need just as the atmosphere filters out harmful rays from the sun.

Guards all around

Not only is the Lord interested in providing sure footing underneath and protection above us, he is prepared to place guards all around us to constantly be there for us in our comings and goings. It is likely that none of us realize how often the Lord has interceded for us. We question why God wasn't there when something bad happens without realizing how many times He was there.

"My help comes from the Lord who made heaven and earth." Ps. 121:2

HOPE

Pastor Jeremy Cook told his Oliver Alliance, BC, congregation about the time he was on Vancouver Island and got up early to go to the

Malahat Summit before sunrise. Waiting in the dark at an isolated viewpoint required patience. A chill in the air added discomfort. A rustling in the nearby bush caused a bit of anxiety until a ferret bounced out, looked at him and left.

Then the sun rose. It painted the sky in a beautiful array of colors. The photography he had come to do paid off. Saanich Bay was unveiled. The view was awesome! What he had hoped for came to be.

Beautiful as it is the world is also marred, polluted and scarred. We also wait for a bright unveiling. The Scriptures offer hope that "*the creation itself will be liberated from its bondage to decay...*" Romans 8:21 Christians can look forward to the time when God will rebuild and restore earth to its original state. He promises a new heaven and a new earth. What a glorious prospect! Don't miss out. Those who acknowledge Jesus as Lord, admit their sinfulness and ask forgiveness will be granted a place by grace. It's a gift.

Grateful to be on the sunny side.

JOSH MCDOWELL

Josh was born into the dysfunctional family of an alcoholic father who had mistreated his mother so much that Josh had even tried to drown him in the bathtub. Part way through law school Josh tried to disprove the resurrection of Christ but in the process became a Christian. His mother had already died by that time. Josh was able to repair relationships with his father and lead him to the Lord but became very troubled about what his mother's spiritual condition had been. During Christmas break from Talbot Seminary in California he became even more disturbed about it. Excerpts in his own words tell the astounding story of what happened.

"I was walking and praying across the near-deserted campus one morning. God, I have no idea how You'll answer this, but I have to ask You. Please let me know whether mom was a believer or not. My heart is burning so much.

On an impulse, I drove to Manhatten Beach – 20 miles away. I parked the car and walked out on the long concrete pier that extended far out into the ocean... At the end of the pier, I leaned out on the railing and looked at the grayish-blue water below....Suddenly I heard a woman's voice. 'I wouldn't do that if I were you...You're not thinking of jumpin', are you? "No, lady, not at all. Just thinking..."

The conversation eventually got around to learning they were both from Michigan.

"I had a cousin who used to live in Michigan", she said... Union City...I was born there," Josh replied. *"What was your cousin's name?" Edith Joslin. She married a man named Wilmot McDowell" ..."Those are my parents!" exclaimed Josh.*

Needless to say both were speechless with astonishment that the two would meet 2000 miles from 'home' on a lonely ocean pier with no one else around.

"I need to ask you a question. Maybe you'll know the answer." "Sure, son." Do you by chance happen to know if my mom ever trusted Christ as Savior and Lord?" "...Your mom and I were just teenagers when a tent revival came to town... And it was the fourth night...that she and I made our decision. We grabbed each other's hand and went forward to accept Christ."

You can imagine Josh's exhileration! Jumping and shouting for joy at the answer to his prayer. It was not a coincidence that just when he desperately needed it, he had headed for <u>this</u> ocean beach, stopped at <u>this</u> pier and conversed with <u>this</u> woman who was his mom's cousin and was the <u>one person</u> who could personally answer his question. God cares very much about His children.

Josh McDowell, Undaunted, 2012, from chapter 19

MULE SENSE

In the 1940's or '50s, the late M.R. DeHaan was invited to conduct a meeting in a remote Kentucky mission station. After alighting from the regular train he transferred to the cab of a logging train that wound around hills and boulders and over rickety bridges. His nervousness was lessened by the engineer who convinced him it would be a safe trip. He made the run daily. When they got within three miles of the mission station he was told that the balance of the trip would be on the back of a mule. He was warned not to use the reins are try to guide the mule. The mule knew the road best. Furthermore, by then it was so dark that Dr. DeHaan couldn't even see the trail. He simply had to trust the mule.

When it was time to return the missionary took him back down the same trail in daylight. M. R. DeHaan almost fainted when he saw what it was like. It was a narrow, dangerous path along the side of the mountain. One misstep could send them 100 feet down into a chasm. He would have been very reluctant to go if he had seen it before on the way up. But the mule was confident and able.

It is best to trust the one who knows the way. Sometimes what we perceive as the way to go is not the wise choice.

The Lord will not lead us on the wrong path.

Source: "Our Daily Bread" Mar. 24, 1964

ONE SOLITARY LIFE

He was born in an obscure village, the child of a peasant woman. He grew up in another village, where he worked in a carpenter's shop until he was thirty. Then for three years he was an itinerant preacher. He never wrote a book, never held an office, never went to college. He never travelled more than two hundred miles from the place where he was born. He did none of the things that usually accompany greatness. He had no credentials but himself. He was only thirty-three when the tide of public opinion turned against him. His friends ran away. One of them denied him. He was turned over to his enemies and went through the mockery of a trial. He was nailed to a cross between two thieves. While dying, his executioners gambled for his clothing, the only property he had on earth. When he was dead, he was laid in a borrowed grave through the pity of a friend ... All the armies that have ever marched, all the navies that have ever sailed, all the parliaments that have ever sat, all the kings that ever reigned put together, have not affected the life of mankind on earth, as powerfully as that one solitary life. He was Jesus.

J.A. Francis, 1926, in The Real Jesus.

OVERFLOWING

Years ago shepherds depended on wells to provide water for their flocks of sheep. Often those wells were deep and the water had to be drawn by hand. That was tedious and hard work. Shepherds who didn't really care about the well-being of the sheep would limit how much water each sheep got, much to the detriment of the sheep. Good shepherds, who loved their sheep, would keep drawing water and even make the large containers overflow to be sure that they all had what they needed. That must be where the imagery in Psalm 23 originated when it says "my cup overflows."

Christ is the Good Shepherd Who does not skimp by doling out stingy portions. He loves to bless us to the point of overflowing with His goodness. God loves us and wants the best for us, but it won't reach us if we ignore or reject Him.

"Taste and see that the Lord is good, blessed is the one who trusts in Him." Psalm 34:8

There is abundance on the sunny side.

RICHES

Imagine that a pastor has been called to the bedside of a wealthy, but very sick, man. He earnestly requested that the pastor pray that he would have his health restored so that he could live. The pastor refuses.

In great consternation the sick asks him why? The answer greatly disturbs him.

"Many people have spurned our church because you come there, enthusiastically sing the songs and go through the motions but it is hypocritical. Your employees complain about unfairness, your family barely tolerates you, and you are unscrupulous with your customers. This community would be better off if you died."

This frank and seemingly brutal approach brought a look of terror to the face of the sick man. If he died now and had to face all that before the Judge of all the earth it would go very badly for him. All his wealth and power would be of no help. It brought him to sincere repentance with many tears. Then the pastor was able to pray for him, he did survive and made big changes in his life.

Truth sometimes hurts before it heals.

TRUST AND TRAGEDY

Louisa Stead, her husband and their daughter, were enjoying a picnic by the ocean. The peaceful and beautiful setting was shattered by the piercing, terrified cry of a young boy. It soon became evident that the lad had been pulled out to sea beyond his depth. He was in danger of drowning. The call for help prompted Mr. Stead to head out into the ocean to help the boy. Panic-stricken, the young lad clung to Mr. Stead in a way that kept him from being able to successfully battle the tide to get back to shore. Both of them drowned as Louisa and her daughter watched helplessly. Her faith in the Lord was severely tested. Grief-stricken, her only source of comfort was to continue placing her trust in the Lord in spite of the devastating circumstances. She found comfort in writing her thoughts down in a poem that began with these words.

'Tis so sweet to trust in Jesus, just to take Him at His word,
Just to rest upon His promise, just to know, "Thus saith the Lord."

The poem was set to music by William Kirkpatrick and became a well-known hymn in many countries of the world.

Not long after this, mother and daughter left to devote themselves to missionary work in South Africa. Twenty-five years of fruitful labor were terminated by her ill health. She died in Southern Rhodesia a few years later. About 5000 native Christians remembered and honored her by singing the song Louisa had written.

A sunny attitude leaves a legacy in spite of harsh trials.

THEME 18

Witnessing

How can I effectively share the good news of the gospel?

"Therefore go and make disciples of all nations, baptizing them in the name of the Father and of the Son and of the Holy Spirit," Matthew 28:19

WHERE'S THE EVIDENCE?

An atheist club had invited a guest speaker who delivered a scathing denunciation of Christians. At the close he challenged anyone to refute his claims. One man arose and told the group that he had been a member of this club for five years but would terminate that membership. He was here to counter the speaker's aim.

Six months ago, he became very ill and lost his job. Not one person from the club came to see him or offer any support. (I would hasten to add that atheists are not generally like that.) The couple who did come to help were Christians whom he had earlier driven away from his place with threats. They cared for his needs and nursed him through his illness. Without that he didn't think he would have survived. He had asked this couple why they would do that for someone who had mistreated them so badly. They replied that the Lord had been kind to them when they had been undeserving and they were just passing it on. Passionately the former atheist concluded his rebuttal with the statement that he had now become a Christian too.

May those of us who claim to be followers of Jesus live up to that standard too. Otherwise our impact will be negative.

BENJAMIN FRANKLIN

In the 18th Century the streets of Philadelphia were dark at night. This made crime and stumbling over obstacles a serious problem. In his autobiography Franklin writes about his frustration with the people for not buying into his idea of placing some kind of lighting outside at night to dispel the problem. No one went to the trouble of trying out the idea. He just couldn't mobilize the people to adopt the idea. Then he hatched a plan. He put a kerosene lantern on a pole outside his own house in such a place that it also cast light on the walkway. People walking by felt safer and didn't stumble in the dark.

Soon another family did the same thing, then another and then still more lit up their own area. Eventually much of the city was lit up by lamps and the problem diminished. He hadn't said a word to anybody, he just set the example.

The lesson is clear. We accomplish more by setting a good example than by exhorting, admonishing or complaining.

HONESTY

The preacher was zealously emphasizing that stealing is very wrong, no matter how small the theft. Keeping what isn't mine is thievery, no excuses. He declared that we need to be absolutely honest in all our dealings.

The next day he boarded a bus where he paid for the fare in paper currency. Back at his seat he discovered that the driver had given him 10 cents too much in change. He double checked his counting. It was indeed too much. He made his way back to the front and told the driver that he had received too much change and was returning the ten cents. The driver told him he had done that on purpose because he was in the audience the day before where he heard the strong message on being honest. The driver declared that if this preacher practices what he teaches I'll come back to hear him again. If he doesn't, I'm through with Christianity.

The driver was back to the church service the following Sunday morning with the conviction that there must be something real about that kind of faith.

Honesty is the best policy.

ICE CREAM

At a recent trip to a restaurant this parent's six-year-old son asked if he could say grace. As they all bowed their heads, he said, "God is good. God is great. Thank you for the food, and I would even thank you more if mom gets us ice cream for dessert. And liberty and justice for all! Amen!" Along with laughter from the other customers nearby, a woman remarked, "That's what's wrong with this country. Kids today don't even know how to pray. Asking God for ice cream! Why, I never!"

Hearing this, the boy burst into tears and asked, "Did I do it wrong? Is God mad at me?" The parent held him and assured him that he had done a terrific job and God was certainly not mad at him. An elderly gentleman approached the table. He winked at the boy and said, "I happen to know that God thought that was a great prayer." "Really?" the boy asked. "Cross my heart," the elderly man replied, and then in a theatrical whisper (loud enough for the woman to hear) the gentleman added, "Too bad she never asks God for ice cream. A little ice cream is good for the soul sometimes."

Naturally, the parent bought the kids ice cream at the end of the meal. The 6 year old stared at his for a moment and then did something the parent will always remember. He picked up his sundae and without a word walked over and placed it in front of the woman. With a big smile he told her, "Here, this is for you. Ice cream is good for the soul sometimes, and my soul is already good."

Love what happens when you stay on the sunny side.

IS THE CHURCH IRRELEVANT?

Many people see the church as boring, untrue and irrelevant. To them it's based on myths, tangled up in superstitions and make belief events. The people in it haggle over doctrinal beliefs and wallow in hypocrisy. It has nothing to say to current life issues. It's a plague and a blight on society.

This deserves a closer look. The church is not a building or an organization, it is more like a living organism. It is God's Plan A for declaring the plan of redemption over the centuries and around the world. Jesus said, "I will build my church". Those who believe in Him are His family. It has had and will continue to be a powerful influence in the world despite faults and warts. It will outlast all efforts to wipe it off the globe and will be the only thing God will salvage from this planet before He makes it all new.

Currently over two billion believers in Jesus Christ form over three million local church groups around the world. We don't know how many secret, "underground" churches there are in addition to these. The church worldwide is growing in spite of persecution that kills up to an estimated 150,000 Christians each year. It involves the biggest participation of volunteers, the strongest motive of love, the simplest administrative plan by using believers where they are gifted to serve and has the unique goal of existing for the benefit of those who are not members.

YOU are invited!!

MUDDY BOOTS

The army sergeant didn't like it that one of the soldiers would kneel by the bed every night to pray. It irked him so much that one night he picked up his muddy boots and threw them at him. One boot hit him on the head and stunned the soldier for a few moments. "Alright," thought the sergeant, "that'll put a stop to him!"

The next day the sergeant found his boots back at his own bed, cleaned and polished. He discovered that the praying soldier had done it. At that point it was the sergeant who was stunned. This was not the expected result. It was the sergeant who was stopped in his tracks, not the soldier. As a result the sergeant decided that he needed what that soldier had, a strong faith in God.

The best sermons are not always ones that are preached in words.

DOES PRAYER EVEN WORK?

"I've tried it and it doesn't work!" is the conclusion of a lot of people. "There's nobody up there listening or even caring about me. Prayer is a futile pursuit." These are responses I've been given by people who asked God to do something and He didn't. When they were told about personal experiences of powerful answers to prayer that I and others have had, they reply that it is just a coincidence. As an example, would you say that the following is a unique coincidence or a powerful answer to prayer?

In the fall of 1853, twenty-one year old Hudson Taylor traveled by sail ship on his first trip to China as a missionary. The ship's route took them very close to a cannibal island. Suddenly the wind died down. This was very dangerous because the ship started drifting toward the island's beach. Cannibals began to gather on the beach, anticipating this meal delivery service. The captain in great distress asked Hudson Taylor to pray for the help of God. "I will", said Taylor, "provided you set the sails to catch the breeze." Youthful Hudson had a strong faith and a clear picture of what God expected of prayer. The captain declined to make himself a laughing stock by unfurling the canvas in a dead calm. Taylor replied, "I will not undertake to pray for the vessel unless you prepare the sails."

Reluctantly the captain yielded to the missionary's wishes. Later, while engaged in prayer, there came a knock on Hudson Taylor's door. "Who is there?" he called. "Are you still praying for wind, Taylor?" "Yes!" "Well, you'd better stop for we have more wind now than we can manage!" At that point they were less than 100 yards from the shore.

Prayer is not an automatic vending machine. It is not a magic medium to get whatever we want. The Bible promises answers for even the weak in faith and the undeserving, but there are also very specific conditions that come into play.

God is more interested in our character than our comfort. That can require the discipline of tough love, even unanswered prayer. See Paul's letter to the Hebrews, chapter 12, verses 5-6.

God is also more concerned about removing moral iniquity than building material equity. Getting more material things is hardly His priority. See Psalm 66:18.

He will also examine our motive. Are we asking for something that will simply cater to our pride or pleasure? See James 4:3. The goodness of God showers us with benefits even if we don't ask for them or are thankful. But sometimes we need tough love.

It is the *"fervent prayer of a righteous person that is powerful and effective"*, according to James 5:16.

TELEMACHUS

In his book, *Loving God*, Charles Colson tells the story of Telemachus, a fourth-century Christian monk. Telemachus lived in a remote village and spent most of his time tending his garden and praying. One day, he sensed that he needed to go to Rome.

The monk responded obediently and set out on foot. Weeks later, he arrived at the city's gates to witness a great festival taking place. He followed the crowd through the streets toward the Colosseum.

Inside, he saw the gladiators stand before the emperor and say, "We who are about to die salute you." Telemachus realized they were going to fight to the death for the entertainment of the crowd, so he cried out, "In the name of Christ, stop!" As the games began, Telemachus pushed through the crowds, climbed over the wall, and dropped to the arena floor screaming over and over, "In the name of Christ, stop!" The crowd thought this was part of the show, so they began laughing. When they realized it wasn't, their laughter turned to angry shouts.

Suddenly, one of the gladiators plunged his sword into the body of Telemachus. (Some historians claim that a group from the spectators stoned him, others say it was both the stoning and the sword.) He fell to the sand and his last words were, "In the name of Christ, stop!" Then, a hush fell over the Colosseum and one man in the upper rows stood up and walked out. Soon, others began to follow and in silence everyone left the Colosseum. On that day, probably in 401 A.D., the last battle to the death between gladiators in the Roman Colosseum was fought. It was all because one tiny voice that could hardly be heard above the uproar spoke the truth in God's name.

One voice can move us toward the sunny side, but it may be at great cost!

THE RESCUING HUG

You may have heard of this event since it made the news nation-wide and was published in Life and in Readers' Digest back in the mid-90's. Twins Brielle and Kyrie were born prematurely to Paul &

Heidi Jackson on Oct. 17, 1995 in Worcester, Mass. At three weeks old two pound Kyrie struggled to breath and was beginning to turn blue. As a last resort nurse Gayle Kasparian went against hospital policy, but with parental permission, to try a practice she had heard of being used in Europe. She placed the failing Kyrie next to Brielle in one incubator. Immediately Kyrie calmed down and began to recover. Brielle had put her arm around the sister she had known in the womb (they had been womb-mates for months). Eventually they grew up and became college students together.

There is healing virtue in a caring touch. I think of the account in the Gospel of Mark where it states that *"People were bringing little children to Jesus to have him touch them, but the disciples rebuked them."* Mar 10:13

We hear a lot on the news about court cases where men have touched women inappropriately. Consequences are just in those cases but let's not forget the touch that cares and heals.

UNASHAMED

A young pastor in Zimbabwe, Africa left this note in his office. It was discovered after this persecuted pastor was found murdered for his faith. Excerpts from the victim's letter appear below.

> *I'm part of the fellowship of the unashamed. ... My past is redeemed, my present makes sense, my future is secure. ... I no longer need preeminence, prosperity, position, promotions, plaudits, or popularity. I don't have to be right, first, tops, recognized, praised, regarded, or rewarded. I now live by faith, lean on his presence, walk by patience, am uplifted by prayer, and labor with power. ... I cannot be bought, compromised, detoured, lured away, turned back, deluded, or delayed. I will not flinch in the face of sacrifice, hesitate in the presence*

*of the enemy, pander at the pool of popularity, or meander in
the maze of mediocrity. ... I am a disciple of Jesus. I must go
till he comes, give till I drop, preach till all know, and work
till he stops me. And, when he comes for his own, he will have
no problem recognizing me...my banner will be clear.*

WOW!! That's a lot to live up to even if we're on the sunny side.

*The incident is recorded in Brennan Manning's
book, The Signature of Jesus.*

WALT'S NEW YEAR

Howie was intent on his game of marbles 'singles' when a shadow
covered him. A tall, lanky fellow greeted him and asked him if he
would be interested in being part of his Sunday School class. Any
sentence with school in it was bad news to Howie. "Not interested,"
he replied. "May I play you a game of marbles?" asked Walt, the
visitor. Now that was better, thought Howie. Walt won every game!
Howie was impressed. He was ready to stick with this guy.

Walt continued on his mission. He had approached his pastor about
being a teacher in the church's Philadelphia Sunday School but there
were no spots available. So the pastor suggested, "If you can recruit
a group of boys from around here we'll find a place where you can
meet with them." Eventually Walt succeeded in gathering 13 boys,
each just under the 'teens. Recalling those times as an adult, Howard
describe this group as a collection of *"ragtag, rough-hewn, cruddy
kids. We became his fans." (Source: "Footprints" 1981 by Howard and
Jeanne Hendricks)*

In addition to class time Walt took the boys on hikes, went sliding
down snowy hills, visited amusement parks, went boating on the
Delaware River and became their friend and confidante. Howie

developed a thirst for making his life significant too. While in sixth grade he decided that he wanted Jesus to be his Savor and then live for Him as Lord. Eventually 11 of the 13 went into vocational Christian work. Walt had introduced these boys to a New Year like no other.

I have read the late Howard Hendricks' books (died Aug. 14, 2019), sat in on one of his seminars and used teaching materials he has developed. What Walt meant to him, Howard Hendricks has been to many others.

That's powerful!

Conclusion

There are many issues that could have been included in these articles but the mandate under which they were written was to emphasize an uplifting and inspirational approach. I hope that this was accomplished in most of them.

As for the more controversial topics, I recognize that very divergent conclusions exist among sincere people. I also admit that some questions we will never know enough about to provide an answer. My conviction about these is to let my life be guided by answers I can't question rather than questions I can't answer.

If you have questions, concerns or wish to respond you may contact me.

Henry G. Wiebe

1203 – 45412 Chehalis Dr.
Chilliwack, BC, Canada V2R 0Y9
1-604-846-7274
lazuli.wiebe@gmail.com

Printed in Canada